Eat, Gay, Love

Calum McSwiggan is a writer and LGBT+ advocate who has worked with charities such as Switchboard, Terrence Higgins Trust and Stonewall. He hosted a popular radio show for FUBAR Radio and has also created several short films, including the award-winning *Love Happens Here*, which was named 'Best LGBT+ Short Film' at the Buffer Festival in Toronto. In 2019 he started a book club to encourage young people to read more LGBT+ literature.

Eat, Gay, Love

Calum McSwiggan

HODDER

First published in Great Britain in 2020 by Hodder & Stoughton
An Hachette UK company

This paperback edition published in 2021

8

Paperback ISBN 978 1 529 38452 9
eBook ISBN 978 1 529 38451 2

Typeset in Sabon MT by Hewer Text UK Ltd, Edinburgh
Printed and bound in Great Britain by Clays Ltd, Elcograf S.p.A.

Hodder & Stoughton policy is to use papers that are natural, renewable
and recyclable products and made from wood grown in sustainable
forests. The logging and manufacturing processes are expected to
conform to the environmental regulations of the country of origin.

Hodder & Stoughton Ltd
Carmelite House
50 Victoria Embankment
London EC4Y 0DZ

www.hodder.co.uk

For Shaun, in hope of a brighter tomorrow.

Author's note

Everything in this story happened as is written, but some of the details, characters and locations have been changed to aid the storytelling process, and to preserve the anonymity of the real-life people the book is based upon.

Readers should note that this book covers content, issues and themes that may potentially be difficult, triggering or upsetting, in particular the Prologue (pages 1 to 5) and Chapters Eight and Nine (pages 105 to 121).

Contents

Prologue

The news would report that the city had lost its humanity for a period of time that day. It was Pride in my hometown, the first one I'd ever attended, and I don't think I'll ever forget the hideous chanting of those crowds. After a long day of celebration, a crowd had gathered around the local shopping centre and they all looked up to the skies as they chanted for the teenage boy to jump. The sound of distant sirens came racing through the air, and police officers blocked my path as I tried to push my way through to see what was happening.

Shaun Dykes tragically lost his life that day and it would be the words of strangers willing him to jump that would be the last thing he'd ever hear. Those words have stuck with me too, and although I never knew Shaun, there's not a day that goes by that I don't think about him and remember his name.

Harvey Milk famously said that all young people, regardless of sexual orientation or identity, deserve a safe and supportive environment in which to achieve their full potential, and Shaun was robbed of that basic human privilege.

As heartbreaking and shocking as a story like this one is, it's not at all uncommon. In fact, LGBT+ teenagers resort to taking their own lives at a disproportionately high rate right across the globe. And it's no surprise when in many towns – just like the one I grew up in – homophobia and transphobia continue to thrive and go unchecked.

That homophobia was the backdrop to the first twenty-two years of my life. Growing up in that small coal mining town wasn't always easy, but I was fortunate and privileged in the fact that I had two loving parents who protected and believed in me. They were the gems among the rubble of the experiences that made me, and it was entirely thanks to them that I was able to grow up feeling unashamed of the person I knew that I was.

It was in that town that I first met Tom. He sat across from me in music class when we were just sixteen years old. Our hands met across the piano as we practised our first duet, and we quickly found ourselves falling head over heels in love.

Tom was far from perfect, but he was the first gay man I ever met – the first person who felt exactly the same as I did – and that bonded us in a way that made it difficult to imagine life without him. So much so that when we finished school and my parents moved away to Spain, I made the difficult decision to stay behind with him.

We didn't have a lot of money, and so when I went to the local university, he took up a job as a scaffolder and lived illegally in my dorm room as he helped to pay my bills. We shared a tiny single bed and ate nothing but fried-egg sandwiches and ramen noodles, but it was the happiest I'd ever been. It was our first taste of independence and after just a couple of years of living together, we were able to rent our own little converted attic that overlooked the only gay bar in town.

We'd peer down into the street below, watching the handful of gay men who would go in and out of the tiny bar each night. It was always the same people. There weren't many queer people in that town, at least not many who were open about it, but we made a couple of LGBT+ friends and would throw little dinner parties, sitting around on cushions on the floor. We couldn't yet afford furniture, but neither of us minded, because as long as we were together it always felt like home.

For five years we mostly lived our lives undisturbed, but every now and then there would be insidious little reminders that we weren't considered equal. People would yell homophobic language in the street, we discovered that we weren't allowed to donate at the local blood drive, and I was even fired from my minimum-wage job after complaining about the homophobia on the factory floor.

Living there and being an out-and-proud gay couple certainly painted a target on our backs, but in spite of all this, Tom still built up the courage to pledge to spend the rest of his life with me. It was my twenty-first birthday when he got down on one knee in front of all of our friends and asked me to marry him. I said yes and we were welcomed into the world as a newly engaged couple to the sound of rapturous applause. I'll never forget the feeling of being lifted into his arms and him kissing me like he'd never kissed me before.

Gay marriage wasn't legal then, but we were still hopeful that things were changing and that the laws would soon catch up with us. We felt unstoppable, but sadly the reality of the world we live in was hard to ignore, and our celebrations were cut short just a few days later when a group of men followed him after work and brutally assaulted him as they tried to force their way into our home. Tom had always been a gentle soul, and it broke my heart to see his hands tremble as I carefully tended to his wounds.

Something changed in us after that. He was now afraid to hold my hand in public, and where we had once defiantly kissed in front of the crowds of protestors at Pride, we now skulked in the shadows and crossed the street whenever we saw someone coming. It took its toll on our relationship, but his fear was definitely warranted, because acceptance of queer people seemed now more distant than ever. Just a few months later the UK's first LGBT+ hate crime convictions were made right there on our doorstep after homophobic leaflets threatening the death penalty had been pushed into every letter box in town. If it wasn't for the LGBT+ people who bravely came forward to speak about how terrifying that was, the perpetrators might have got away with it, too.

It may be hard to believe that so many terrible things could happen in one little town, but the truth is that most LGBT+ people have stories exactly like these ones. Despite the enormous progress we've made in recent years, queer people from all over the world are still at risk of being discriminated against every single day.

My relationship with Tom never really recovered and, after five and a half years, it fell apart. I'd thought I would probably stay in that town for ever, but after graduation, I went away to Italy for the summer to teach English, and although the time apart had made my love for him stronger, I returned home to find he'd fallen in love with somebody else. A tan line still lingered on my finger for months after I gave my ring back, and I was relegated to sleeping on the sofa while I listened to him fucking his new boyfriend in the next room. All the while hanging on and holding out that one day he'd come back to me. He didn't. And after nine painful months I'd finally had enough. I sold all my possessions, packed everything into a single suitcase and left.

I was tempted to retreat to my parents' home in Spain, but I was determined to do things on my own, and so I went back to the job in Italy that I'd left behind the previous summer. I knew I wouldn't stay there for ever, but I had to start somewhere, and it was the last place I remembered being happy.

Saying goodbye to my hometown was the most difficult part. That town may have been grey and dreary and a little rough around the edges, but it was the place where I'd grown up, and was home to every single memory I'd ever made. Childhood adventures, tree-houses and campfires. Drinking games in my university dorm room. Graduation and countless nights dancing in the student bar. My first kiss and holding hands and saying yes as Tom got down on one knee. My whole life had been there, and just like that, it was gone.

It was the most difficult decision I had ever made, but I knew that there had to be something better than this. I took a deep breath as the bus to the airport pulled out and away from the city, and as I watched my hometown fade into the distance, I promised myself that I would never come back.

ITALY

ITALY

Chapter One

He let out a soft sigh as he wrapped his naked arms around me and pulled me in closer, his sticky skin pressing against mine as his sweet breath caressed the back of my neck. I rolled over to face him, his lips barely an inch away from mine, and with closed eyes we lay there silently, each knowing that the other was only pretending to be asleep.

His name was Matteo. He had sharp cheekbones, tousled black hair and freckles on each cheek. I was twenty-two and he was nineteen, and even though I'd only known him for a few days, I absolutely adored him. He drew his face a little closer to mine, and he swallowed hard as his eyelids fluttered open and we caught each other's stare. All I could think about was how badly I wanted to kiss his trembling lips, but while this may well have been the closest he'd ever come to kissing another boy, tonight wasn't going to be the night.

I know that many gay men have stories exactly like this one. Stories of teenage lust, uncertain sexuality and curious hands. But the thing is, none of this was new to me then, because I'd done all this before. When I stepped out of the closet and into a relationship with Tom, I never thought for one moment that I'd ever go back in. Yet here I was, hiding in the shadows, in a small rustic town just outside of Rome.

The sound of the front door opening downstairs cut through the silence. Matteo and I rolled away from one another in frustration, hearts racing as we listened to his father's footsteps climbing the stairs. We weren't doing anything wrong by being here; in fact, it was his father who had suggested it. He'd welcomed me into his home, offered to feed me and take care of me and, although he had a perfectly viable sofa bed downstairs, had insisted that his eldest son's bed would be the best place for me to sleep.

His name was Giuseppe and he was the epitome of a typical Italian man. He had short unmade hair and stubble, and although he was quite small in height, his broad shoulders and strong posture made him seem all that much bigger. He had a temper and was quick to raise his voice, but he was kind and genuine and his love for his family was unwavering. He ran his own construction business but frequently took time off to spend at home because, to him, family meant everything. He always greeted his two sons with the warmest of embraces, and he kissed his wife with such passion that it made you feel like you had to turn and look away. His wife's name was Ornella, and together they were a powerhouse, two parents that anyone would feel incredibly lucky to have.

Ornella was a slender woman who made you wonder where she was putting the mountains of food that she prepared for us. She always had her curly hair tied back in a messy bun, ready to roll up her sleeves and start work on her latest feast. Her English was perfect, but she encouraged me to speak Italian with her anyway, and celebrated every single word I got correct. I always felt safe with her. She very much reminded me of my own mother, and I knew that she could never do me or her family any wrong.

The school I'd been assigned to teach in had paired me up with them, and they offered to let me live with them rent-free in exchange for tutoring their youngest. His name was Lorenzo; he had been adopted from Cambodia and they described him as the missing puzzle piece to their family. At four years old he was loud and boisterous and always had to make his presence known. They'd tried to explain that he was adopted but he was too young to understand, and when asked where Cambodia was, he would say it was the place where babies came from. His mother would watch all of this and clap her hands together and smile, and smile, and smile. Forever proud of her wonderful family, and willing to go to the ends of the earth to make sure that they were happy.

We lived in our own little world. The food was served, the wine was poured and Matteo's warm body would press up against me each night. It would have all been perfect if it wasn't for our secret. None of the others knew that either of us were gay, and I'm pretty sure that Giuseppe would have wrung my neck if he'd walked in on me with my arms around his son.

'Open your eyes,' somebody whispered, shaking me gently. It was a few days earlier and I'd awoken to find myself sitting on the parked train, having just arrived in Rome. The kind stranger smiled and said something in Italian before lifting up her suitcase and disappearing down the aisle. Her hair bounced with multicoloured curls as she went, and I noticed a rainbow sticker on her bag just as she slipped out of the door.

It was a welcome surprise because I'd always been a little unsure about Italy's relationship with the LGBT+ community. If there's one thing I'd learned from the previous summer I'd spent here, it was that it always felt as if the country's LGBT+ residents were kept hidden behind closed doors. I'd been out to some of Rome's underground gay clubs and the famous 'Gay Street Di Roma' – and although those spaces may have given the impression of a liberally progressive society, things weren't that simple if you looked a little deeper. Seeing somebody so visibly queer outside of those spaces was, in my experience, a rarity – and although I'd never witnessed any outright homophobia, it sometimes felt like there was something bubbling just below the surface.

I'd befriended a pair of gay twins the last time I'd been here. They'd come out to their parents just two days apart, and although their parents didn't outwardly reject them, they turned a blind eye to their homosexuality and acted as if it simply didn't exist. They told me that this kind of queer erasure wasn't exactly uncommon, and that they believed most of it could be attributed to the influence of religion throughout the country.

Rome's close proximity to the Vatican meant that this influence was noticeably felt. The streets were often filled with groups of smiling nuns and friendly priests, and for the most part they seemed harmless – you might even say endearing. The problem came when the conversations turned to LGBT+ equality. It would be those bound to the Catholic Church who would be the first to attend the protests, to speak out, to prevent the same progress that had been made elsewhere. Their presence was so overwhelming that it made it impossible for even the most liberal political parties to ignore them, and so LGBT+ advancements had been stunted, indefinitely frozen in time.

Even my employers were very clear on the fact that I was not to disclose my sexuality to my students or the families I'd be sent to live with. They argued that it wasn't relevant and that there was no reason to bring it up, but from experience I knew full well that every Italian mother would be quizzing me about my romantic life the moment I walked through the door. I'd had to take off my engagement ring because it invited too many questions, and if anything, I was grateful that I no longer had that to worry about.

In spite of all this, things were certainly getting better – queer activists like Vladimir Luxuria were bringing LGBT+ people into the mainstream. She was the first openly transgender member of parliament in Europe, and she made a difference not just by forging a political identity, but by working as an actress and a TV presenter and helping many Italians to understand queerness in a way they hadn't before.

The serendipitous celebration that awaited me that day suggested that perhaps these efforts were working, and that change was indeed happening in Italy. The girl from the train wasn't alone – Pride had come to the city just in time for my arrival, and all of Rome seemed to have been submerged in a sea of rainbows. Revellers decked out in glistening heels and crop tops filled the station, and people of all ages blew whistles and cheered on each and every corner. There were people carrying signs emblazoned with messages of solidarity, and others embraced as they came from all over the country to join each other in celebration.

It was remarkable that this was how my adventure started, and I wish I could've stayed and enjoyed the festivities a little longer, but it was there, in the most unlikely of places, that I met Giuseppe for the first time.

Standing outside the station alone, looking bewildered by the spectacle, he waited patiently by his car with a big cardboard sign that had my name on it.

'Nice to meet you,' he said, taking my hand and shaking it for an eternity before kissing me on both cheeks and excitedly pulling me into his car. '*Parli italiano, no?*' he asked. 'No problem, no problem,' he continued, snatching an Italian phrasebook from his glovebox and shoving it into my hands.

It was a long drive out into the countryside, and as I relaxed into the passenger seat I watched the crowds of marching people fade into the peaceful quiet of miles of rolling greenery. I was a little disappointed that I was being snatched away from the queer celebrations that had awaited me, but I tried to remind myself that Pride wasn't actually what I was here for, and I was just grateful to have been picked up by someone who so quickly made me feel at home. Giuseppe didn't say much as we drove, but he occasionally pointed to things through the window and smiled to himself as if he, too, were seeing all of this for the first time. There were no other cars on the roads, and as we drove away from the city I wondered which of the scattered country houses and villas I would call home for the next few months. It was liberating not knowing where I was going and to put my complete trust in a total stranger. It was a welcome distraction from the memory of everything I was leaving behind.

The house was everything I imagined it would be. It made up in character for what it distinctly lacked in size, with speckled brickwork and wild vines climbing every surface. It overlooked nothing but sloping hills and vineyards, and the branches of the tall olive trees curled and twisted and hid it away from the neighbouring houses. Carefully manicured hedges lined the driveway out front, freshly felled blood oranges scattered the garden path and a vintage Alfa Romeo sat in the open garage alongside a little red Vespa.

The inside of the home smelled like risotto and fresh basil; jars of pasta lined the kitchen shelves, and hanging plant pots stuffed with fragrant herbs bathed in the sunlight that beamed in through the big open windows. Ornella greeted me with open arms as we arrived, and before we could be properly introduced she insisted that we sit down to eat.

'*Mangia*, eat,' she encouraged, plating up some fresh buffalo mozzarella and pushing it in front of me before returning to preparing her home-made arancini. Giuseppe helped by cutting up pizza with a pair of scissors and Lorenzo came scampering to the table to join us. Giuseppe lifted him up onto his seat and he looked at me with excitement and wonder, as if he were waiting for me to perform. I gave him a little wink and stuck out my tongue. He exploded into a fit of giggles, hiding behind his tiny hands and peering out from between his fingers. I didn't know what else to do or say, and knowing Italians aren't shy about their food, I grabbed a slice of pizza and began to eat.

Giuseppe mirrored me by grabbing a slice himself just as his beautiful teenage son came bumbling down the stairs. He was wearing nothing but a ripped pair of blue Levi's, and his hair was still matted and wet from the shower. I smiled nervously in his direction, not knowing where to look as he snatched a T-shirt from a hamper of dirty clothes and pulled it over his slender body.

'Matteo!' Giuseppe rose to embrace him. 'You must meet your new brother.'

'*Piacere*,' I said, getting up from my seat and holding out my hand.

'Really nice to meet you,' he said, laughing, playfully slapping away my hand and pulling me in for a hug. He spoke perfect English, with a soft Italian lilt. 'I don't know if my dad mentioned, but we'll be sharing a room together. I hope that's okay?'

'Fine with me,' I gulped, my heart quickening at the thought.

'I'm going to be working in your school, too. I'll be around to help out, whatever you need.' Having attended the summer school himself when he was younger, Matteo now volunteered as a teacher's assistant, and had been assigned to work with me. He sat down next to his father, who began rattling off in Italian.

'So, you have a girlfriend?' Ornella asked, as we sat side by side at the table.

'I'm single,' I said, honestly surprised it had taken her this long to ask the question.

'*Non è vero!* A handsome man like you? Well, maybe a nice Italian girl then?' She winked and I smiled, a little uncomfortably. If it were up to me, I would have ignored my employer and told them there and then. Part of me wished that I did, because I missed my opportunity, and that was the last chance I'd get.

Matteo and Giuseppe were deep in conversation and, although I couldn't understand what they were saying, I noticed that Giuseppe's warm and friendly tone was starting to shift and that his hand gestures were becoming more erratic. His soft voice turned harsh, and suddenly it was clear he wasn't happy. It sounded like he was complaining and I was afraid that it would be about me.

'*Tutto bene?*' I said, forcing a smile. 'Everything okay?'

'It's fine, don't worry,' Matteo reassured me. 'He's just complaining about how busy it was in town. It shouldn't have taken so long to pick you up.'

I immediately thought of the flourish of rainbow colours I'd seen on my arrival, and Giuseppe continued to complain, shaking his head and waving his hands with annoyance.

'Dad. *Basta*,' Matteo warned. 'Stop.'

'I don't like,' Giuseppe said harshly after a few moments of silence, pushing his plate away from him. But I knew he wasn't talking about the food.

I said nothing and smiled weakly as I reached for another pizza slice, and that's when he mumbled something in Italian that made Ornella wince.

'What did he say?' I asked, but the colour had already drained from Matteo's face.

'It doesn't matter,' he said, waving me away and trying to change the subject.

'No, really, what did he say?' I pressed, and Matteo sighed with apologetic sadness.

'He said gay people make him sick.'

Chapter Two

It was dark when I woke up, and Matteo was still asleep on my chest. It had been three days since Giuseppe had made those comments, but I still couldn't shake his words from my mind.

Giuseppe was, in every other capacity, a deeply kind and compassionate man, and yet he had this homophobic underbelly that made me feel unnerved just to be in his presence. It's easy to be angry when someone yells homophobic language at you in the street, but it's a lot harder to sustain that anger when a smiling face is sitting opposite you, putting food on your plate and giving you a warm bed to sleep in. In a lot of ways, it's the silent homophobia that's worse. It demands your tolerance, seems forgivable and unthreatening and yet feels just as crushing for the people who have to endure it.

Matteo and I didn't speak about that night, carrying on and acting as if his father had never said anything at all, but I think it was those words that ultimately pushed him into my arms. It wasn't an act of rebellion or defiance – that wasn't in Matteo's nature – but I think he saw me as a life raft, that he was drowning in this small isolated town and I was somebody to hold on to.

I ran my fingers through his hair and he sighed softly as he began stirring awake. I knew that this intimacy could only exist in the dead of the night, and so I savoured the moments before we'd be forced to get up and return to reality. Sure enough, the rattling of his alarm jolted us apart, almost as if nothing had happened at all.

'*Buongiorno*,' he said sleepily as he climbed out of bed with a yawn. He made his way across the room to open the curtains, his white Calvin Klein briefs hugging his waist perfectly, his hipbones jutting out in a way that only encouraged me to stare.

He grabbed a clean pair of underwear from his drawer, pulled off the ones he was wearing and turned round so the full picture of his boyish nakedness faced me.

'*Tutto bene?*' he said casually, pulling on the clean briefs, willingly oblivious to my flushed cheeks and wandering eyes. I gave him a half-smile and a little nod as he reached his hand down to rearrange himself before flashing me a mischievous and cheeky grin. His carefree attitude screamed trouble, and yet he had a certain nice-guy innocence that meant, at least in my eyes, that he could do no wrong.

He disappeared to take a shower, and when he came back the first signs of sunlight were beginning to break through the window behind him. It illuminated his surprisingly muscular torso as he stood in front of the mirror, tousling his unmade hair this way and that. 'Are you not getting up?' he asked, looking at my reflection in the mirror as I tried to cover the morning erection stirring beneath the sheets.

'In a minute.' I blushed as he gave me a knowing look.

'*Va bene*,' he said, pulling on an oversized baseball jersey before heading downstairs to make coffee.

He was singing along to 'Hotel California' by the Eagles when I finally got up, showered and made my way down to join him. His voice was sweet and off-key, and the way he loudly sang the mispronounced words showed his obliviousness to the fact that everyone was still sleeping. American TV had definitely had an impact on him, and sometimes when he spoke he sounded to me like something straight out of a nineties sitcom.

'Cappuccino?' he called as I sleepily sat myself down at the kitchen table. I shook my head. 'But it's your first day of work, surely you must have a coffee?' He cocked his head to one side, confused by the illogical foreigner, before turning back to the coffee pot as it came to the end of its boil. He poured me a cup anyway and sat opposite me, the coffee cups warming our hands as the morning sun filled the room around us.

'You have taught before, no?' he asked. I nodded, thinking back to the previous summer I'd spent here. I explained how I'd been engaged, how it had been hard to maintain a long-distance relationship, and how I'd written to Tom every single day.

'*Francobolli*,' I said. It was one of the first Italian words I'd ever learned. 'Stamps. I was always buying stamps.'

'I've never met a gay dude before,' he finally said after a pause, casually licking rogue drops of coffee from his fingertips. 'There's not many people like you around here at all.' It was the first time he'd acknowledged it out loud, and although deep down I already knew that he knew, a big part of me still held onto the secret. I said nothing and took another sip as Giuseppe appeared at the top of the stairs.

'*Buongiorno*,' he said, beaming, coming down into the kitchen and placing one hand on each of our shoulders. My body tensed up at his touch, but I smiled politely and said good morning anyway. It wasn't that I disliked him; in fact, it was quite the opposite, but feeling like I had to hide who I was made me anxious whenever he was in the room.

'We'd better go,' Matteo interrupted, clearly picking up on my signals, as he drained the remnants of his cappuccino from his mug and rose to his feet. 'Don't wanna be late for your first day.' He tossed me an apple and a pastry and grabbed the keys to his Vespa. 'Ready?'

'*In bocca al lupo*,' Giuseppe said as I stood up. I smiled back at him despite the fact I didn't have any idea what that meant. We just didn't understand each other yet.

'Something about a wolf?' I whispered to Matteo and he laughed and told me not to worry about it.

'*Ciao papà*,' he called and led me out of the front door.

It was the classic Italian cliché but there was something truly special about perching on the back of Matteo's Vespa as he whizzed us through the countryside. I'd tried to catch hold of his jacket as I hopped on the back, but he responded with the distinctive Italian '*no*' and took my hands, placing them firmly around his waist. A safety precaution, no doubt, but something I interpreted as an attempt to be closer to me, nonetheless. It seemed so strange that this confident young man was the same nervous teenager who'd been lying next to me for the past three nights – the same boy who'd stripped naked in front of me so confidently that morning, and yet quivered at even the slightest night-time touch.

I felt like a giddy and reckless teenager speeding around town like this. The sweetness of the cologne he'd splashed on his neck drew me to hold him closer, but part of me worried about being so overt with my affections. There couldn't have been many more than a few hundred people in that town, and the equally charming and invasive thing about living in small-town Italy was that everyone knew your business.

Italians are very tactile people, though, so there was an element of hiding in plain sight when I held on to him like this. As he sped well beyond the legal speed limit, I pressed myself up against him, my lips a fraction of an inch away from his neck. I allowed my hands to slip underneath his jacket and, resting them on his hipbones, I let the tips of my thumbs disappear into the top of his jeans.

Absolutely nothing in this town was within walking distance, and so with no transport of my own, I became reliant on Matteo for everything. He became my own personal ferryman and took me everywhere without complaint. At home with his dad he was my translator; on the roads he was my driver, and at school he was my assistant. He'd sit on the cabinets at the back of the classroom and watch me attempt to teach, contentedly kicking his legs with that frustratingly compelling grin plastered across his face. He had the attention span of an excitable puppy and was a distraction more than anything, but all the same he served as a beacon of moral support and I appreciated his company. We'd often take the students out to the back of the school for a game of football or capture-the-flag when we were supposed to be teaching them sentence structure; we were quite possibly the most irresponsible teaching duo the school had ever seen, but the kids were happy, the parents were happy and we were happy, too.

'Do you have a girlfriend?' Ginevra, one of my students, asked on my second week of teaching, pushing back her long ginger hair with a smirk. At fourteen, Ginevra was one of the oldest and one of my favourite students, intelligent beyond her years but also a notorious troublemaker.

The class giggled. At first I thought she was talking to Matteo, but she – and the entire class – had all turned to look at me. I hesitated; I could have easily told them that it was none of their business, and maybe I should have, but something in that moment made me want to tell them the truth. Matteo looked at me with wide eyes from the back of the room, and I think it was his being there that encouraged me to say what I wanted to. My silence would have indicated that there was something wrong with being gay, that it was something to be hidden and to be ashamed of, and I just couldn't do that to him.

I certainly couldn't do that to my students.

'I don't have a girlfriend, no.' I smiled. 'I had a fiancé once, but it didn't work out.'

'Was she pretty?' Ginevra pushed, unsatisfied with the answer.

'*He* was very handsome, yes,' I said, looking to Matteo for approval as the image of Tom danced across my mind. I took a piece of chalk and tried to divert their attention. 'Why don't we draw our ideal partners and label them with the attributes we would like them to have?' I drew a stickman on the board and scrawled '*intelligent*', '*adventurous*' and '*handsome*' alongside it.

The class stared at me blankly for a moment. I waited for them to take it in, to say something, but they didn't. The revelation wasn't anywhere near as shocking as I'd anticipated; in fact, they barely blinked.

'Big breasts!' fifteen-year-old Giovanni shouted with excitement, breaking through the silence as he snatched up his pencil and got straight to work. 'And a very nice bikini,' he concluded.

'Well, maybe let's focus more on her personality.' I laughed nervously, imagining angry parents descending on the school and demanding I be stripped of my job. It wasn't something I'd ever really thought about before – losing my job – because although I'd always bent the rules slightly with my teaching methods, this was the first time I'd ever outright broken them. I was certain it was the right thing to do, however, because I don't think you ever really get over the damage that's done when you're raised to believe that there's something fundamentally wrong with you.

I grew up in a world where the very people who were there to teach and educate me were forbidden from telling me otherwise. Section 28, put in place by Margaret Thatcher's government in 1988, was a legal amendment that prevented homosexuality from being 'promoted' in schools, and it caused an untold amount of damage to entire generations of LGBT+ kids. It was overturned in my late teens, but the legacy of fear it left behind would continue to silence conversations for years to come.

Luckily – and quite surprisingly – no such law ever existed here in Italy, and so I wasn't about to let those conversations be silenced here, too. There weren't really any questions from my students, though, and it was a relief to watch them feverishly working away on their ideal partners, entirely unfazed by my revelation, as I walked around the class correcting their spelling and making alternative suggestions to some of the filth and profanity they'd scribbled down. That's the remarkable thing about young minds – they're not prejudiced by default.

'What was his name?' Ginevra finally asked, as I stopped by her desk and examined her drawing of a tall dark-skinned man in a suit. She'd written '*big muscles*' and '*big wallet*' next to him in enormous decorative writing.

'That's none of your business,' I said with a laugh, looking more closely at her drawing. 'And what about his personality?' I raised my eyebrow and tapped my pencil on her picture.

'Oh, he has a very big personality.' She snickered. 'A really very big personality.'

'I bet he does,' I said disapprovingly, as Matteo laughed from the back of the room.

'You did good today,' Matteo said that evening after dinner, appearing in the doorway as I sat on the end of his bed marking the ridiculous drawings. 'Do you want to go into Rome tonight?'

I looked up and found him standing there wet and wearing nothing but a towel tied lazily around his waist. A tuft of wiry black hair crawled up towards his belly button, tempting me to look down.

'Sure, I guess,' I said, as Matteo closed the door behind him.

'Then you'd better shower too. You need it.' He snatched the towel from around his waist, throwing it at me as he walked across the room. His lack of shame around his body was incredibly

European, but his eagerness to constantly strip off in front of me suggested that he knew exactly what he was doing.

He wasn't wrong, though; I really did need that shower. The heatwave that summer was so unbearable that the Italians had named it Lucifer. It made the air unbreathable, and the thermometer in the town centre had all but given up, and now just displayed zeros. I was hot and I was sweaty and I was so unbelievably horny. I hadn't had sex since my break-up all those months ago, and the constant barrage of sweet Italian accents and exposed olive skin was starting to take its toll. I'd talked to a few guys on Grindr – it was a great way to practise my Italian – 'Si sono pasivo', 'Ti faccio un pompino?' – but all of them were miles away in Rome and it wasn't as if I could just sneak out of the house unnoticed.

I tidied away the drawings I'd been marking and put them neatly by the side of Matteo's bed, and then unlocked my suitcase to take out some clean underwear.

'I'll be right back,' I said, trying not to stare at Matteo's body as I made my way out of the door and down the hall to the bathroom. There was only one bathroom for the whole family; it was small and humid, and the tiny window only let in the faintest bit of light. It was the least sexy place I'd ever been, but with the thought of Matteo in my mind, I made quick work of what would have usually taken at least five or six minutes. I closed my eyes and, biting down hard on my bottom lip, let all my inappropriate thoughts wash away down the drain.

It was a relief but it felt wrong, like a betrayal to Giuseppe and Ornella, to think about their son this way. Despite Giuseppe's hate-filled words, I was a guest in his home, and I still felt a strange fondness for him. I wasn't sure how much longer I could hide the fact that I was gay, and lusting for Matteo right under his nose felt like I was playing with fire. But how very tempting that fire was.

I washed my hair and, intending to play Matteo at his own game, made my way back to his bedroom wearing nothing but the towel around my waist. My heart pounded as I slowly pushed open the bedroom door and, expecting to see Matteo waiting there, gasped when I saw I had another visitor instead.

'*Ciao bello!*' Lorenzo shouted excitedly, turning away from my suitcase to face me. And that's when it hit me. There was a reason why I usually kept my suitcase locked and away from prying eyes, and that reason was now in Lorenzo's hand.

My mind jumped to all the stories Giuseppe had told me about how much they loved their youngest son, and how they went to the ends of the earth to adopt him – and here he was, waving around one of my sex toys. It was a replica mould of Tom's penis. He'd given me a clone-a-willy kit as a joke present and I didn't have the heart to throw it away after we separated. It was clean and unused, but even still I could only imagine Giuseppe's horror if he walked in and found his precious son stood here like this. The terror of this being the way he found out about my sexuality left me frozen to the spot.

Hours seemed to pass as I stood there, watching the sex toy waving around in slow motion. Then, with lightning adrenaline coursing through my veins, I darted across the room and snatched it out of Lorenzo's hand, slamming it down into the suitcase. My sudden outburst caused Lorenzo to burst into a fit of tears, and he kept saying something in Italian I couldn't understand.

'It's okay, it's okay, I'm sorry,' I said, kneeling down to his level in a panic and placing my hands on his shoulders. 'Everything's okay, Lorenzo, I'm sorry.'

He continued crying and began speaking faster and faster, before freeing himself of my grip and running downstairs, no doubt to inform his mother of the monster that I was.

'*Mama!*' he screamed with a hint of bloody murder as his little feet scampered into the kitchen, where Ornella was sat with a toolbox fixing the sink.

'*Cucciolo*,' she said with great worry, kneeling down to embrace him. It was her pet name for him, literally meaning 'puppy'; it suited him. He cried and he cried and as he told her what happened she looked more and more puzzled.

'You have a toy he wants to play with?' She turned to me, shrugging her shoulders. I was still stood wearing nothing but a towel. My lips trembled and I shook my head.

'No, I don't know. I don't have anything,' I lied, unable, in my panic, to come up with a reasonable explanation and wishing I had kept my suitcase locked shut.

She shrugged again and began soothing the boy with sweet Italian utterances as Matteo came through the door. 'What's going on?' he asked, turning to me and looking puzzled as if wondering why I was stood in the kitchen wearing nothing but a towel.

'I don't know, Lorenzo was in your room and then he was crying and—'

'What's up, little man?' Matteo scooped Lorenzo up onto his shoulders before repeating the question in his mother tongue. Lorenzo giggled and whispered something, pointing in my direction.

'He says you've got something in your suitcase – a game, or something?'

'Oh, no, I don't know . . .' I trailed off helplessly as Lorenzo began wriggling free from Matteo's grasp, heading for the stairs the second his brother set him down.

'Come back, Lorenzo!' Ornella called. The boy ignored her, heading up towards Matteo's bedroom and my still-unlocked suitcase. Matteo followed him up the stairs and I followed closely behind. I imagined every worst possible outcome as I reached the bedroom and saw Lorenzo once again rifling through my things. My heart thumped with every item of clothing he moved aside, frantically tearing through and desperately looking for a toy that he didn't know was only supposed to be for adults.

He pulled one of my jumpers aside and there it was, the tip poking out from beneath the clothes. That was when Ornella pushed in from behind me. 'There's nothing there, Lorenzo,' she said, scooping him up from the floor and carrying him out of the room. 'You must have imagined it. Stay out of Calum's things, okay?'

I pulled the suitcase shut, threw the padlock back on and took a deep sigh of relief. I couldn't help but think how Giuseppe would have reacted if he'd come in and found his four-year-old son stood there with a sex toy – a sex toy belonging to the gay man sharing a bed with his eldest son.

'I know what was in your suitcase.' Matteo laughed. He had taken me out to the city for drinks that evening, joined by two of his boisterous, vulgar-mouthed friends, Gabriele and Gianmarco. Matteo supervised while the three of us drank every last drop of wine that Rome had to offer.

'I don't know what you're talking about.' I blushed, and he generously let me change the subject. He had been the perfect gentleman all evening, picking up the bill at *aperitivo* and then guiding us through the streets as we went from bar to bar. He didn't touch a drop himself so that he could drive us all home safely, and he remained eternally patient with Gabriele and Gianmarco's relentless drunken mockery.

They'd been friends with Matteo since school, but their personalities were so at odds with his – they were loud and mischievous and constantly in fits of laughter, and were dead set on causing trouble everywhere they went. Some of my students were better behaved than these two, but Matteo loved them anyway, and affectionately described them as '*pagliacci*' – a pair of clowns.

I felt a lot more relaxed here in Rome, and although it was clear that Matteo's sexuality had never been discussed, I wasn't afraid to be open about who I was. It was easy to get lost here in the city – everyone was a stranger, and nobody knew your business. Gabriele and Gianmarco were cool with it too. It seemed to be a lot more accepted among the younger generations and, much like my students, they were completely unbothered by the revelation. They even tried to figure out what my type was, pointing out passing guys they thought I'd find attractive. Everyone they pointed at was much older and more masculine in appearance than I'd ordinarily go for, but I smiled and went along with it anyway, not wanting to confess that I liked guys who were a little younger and less outwardly masculine – guys a little more like Matteo.

'And what about you?' I finally asked, turning the question back on them as we settled on a dilapidated fountain with one last bottle of wine. Matteo stayed quiet, but Gabriele and Gianmarco enthusiastically began regaling us with tales of their sexual conquests. They were clearly trying to outdo each other with their stories, but the way Matteo rolled his eyes suggested that what they were saying wasn't entirely true.

'What about your girlfriend?' Gianmarco finally said to Matteo, who shot him a look that suggested he really didn't want to talk about it. The pair of them burst into quickfire Italian and Gianmarco giggled as Matteo swiped at him playfully.

'She is not real,' Gabriele whispered to me as the other two continued to fight. His English was good but he always spoke in short, staccato sentences. 'We have never met her. We have never seen the pictures. Where are the pictures, Matteo?'

'Her name is Silvia,' Matteo quipped back. 'And she is real.'

'Her name was Francesca two weeks ago,' Gianmarco teased, messing up Matteo's hair.

'I think that's enough wine for the both of you,' Matteo replied, trying to laugh it off. He stood up and reached for the bottle but Gabriele snatched it away. I laughed as I watched the three of them fighting, but I couldn't help feeling a pang of jealousy rising in my stomach. It didn't really matter whether Matteo's girlfriend was real – even the thought of him being with someone else made me jealous. I'd had him to myself this whole time, and now suddenly I was faced with the very real possibility that Matteo might have a girlfriend, and that he might be bisexual, or even straight.

We have a tendency to oversimplify sexuality sometimes, but it's not at all unusual for straight men to experiment with other guys, or even for gay men to experiment with women. For me, it was my best friend in high school, my first schoolboy crush, and he's now happily married to a woman and has kids. I thought he liked me back, but he didn't – it can be incredibly easy to mistake someone's curious nature for them reciprocating feelings, and I couldn't help but wonder if I was making that same mistake with Matteo.

'*Andiamo?*' he finally said, retrieving the now-empty bottle from Gabriele, who was looking pleased with himself after having drained the remaining drops.

'*Vento*,' Gianmarco agreed. 'Like the wind.'

I tried to join them and stood up. The wine rushed to my head and I stumbled forward over one of the many cobblestones lining the street. Matteo caught me and steadied me, shooting the boys a disapproving look as they giggled at my intoxication.

'I knew I shouldn't have let you have that extra bottle,' he said, guiding me down a winding street glowing prettily with fairy lights and candlelit doorways. Someone was playing 'Volare' on an accordion in the distance and the boys bounced around us, singing along at the top of their lungs.

'*Sono ubriaco*,' I said, trying to impress him with my Italian. 'I'm drunk.'

'*Sì*,' he said with a laugh. '*Molto ubriaco*. Let's get you something to eat.' He pointed ahead to a bakery that was still open despite the fact that we were fast approaching 2 a.m. There was a line of fellow drunks snaking out of the open doorway, and the warmth of the roaring bread oven hit us before we could even get close.

Italians love their food and no meal was an exception – drunken Americans may eat McDonalds and drunken Brits, kebabs, but the Italians wouldn't settle for anything less than freshly baked focaccia. Warm doughy carbs sprinkled with fresh herbs and rock salt, lightly dusted with Parmesan and filled with mozzarella and prosciutto. I let Matteo order for me and he pushed the layered bread into my hands, smiling as I bit down into gooey, olive-oil-soaked goodness, before drunkenly wolfing down the whole thing.

I was truly falling in love with this wonderful country – with its food, and with the boy who had so kindly bought it for me.

After I had contentedly filled my stomach with carbs, Matteo put his arm around me to guide me on. I let myself shrink into him as he pulled me in a little closer, and my heart swelled three sizes as he slid his hand down to meet mine. I didn't know what it meant; perhaps all of this was just a sign of friendship. Neither Gabriele nor Gianmarco seemed to so much as bat an eyelid when they noticed us holding hands. Perhaps they thought nothing of it. Perhaps we were once again hiding in plain sight, or perhaps the two of them were just way more aware of Matteo's sexuality than they ever let on. I hadn't held another boy's hand since Tom, and even he had been afraid to do so in public after everything that had happened to him. And so it was there in Rome, with a boy who may have been unsure of his sexuality, that I walked hand in hand with another man for the first time in as long as I could remember.

It didn't last long, however – it never does. Matteo quickly withdrew his hand as soon as we turned a corner onto a busy street.

There's an uncomfortable feeling of rejection that comes with having someone let go of you like that. You understand why; you're entirely sympathetic, and yet it stings all the same. That familiar feeling of shame rushing back as you realise you're still not entirely free to be yourself. It's something that's seldom talked about because, perhaps, it's something we simply get used to. Hand-holding is a privilege so often reserved exclusively for straight people, and I don't think I've ever held someone's hand in a crowded place without feeling a little bit of discomfort, or as if everyone's watching.

Matteo didn't hold my hand again until we were safely back inside the privacy of his bedroom, his father sleeping soundly at the other end of the hall. I drunkenly climbed into bed beside Matteo and found his hand beneath the blankets. I wrapped my fingers tightly around his and that was all the contact I needed. It almost didn't matter that we couldn't be with one another anywhere else, because we could always be with each other here.

Chapter Three

My head was still pounding from the night before as Matteo drove me to school, and the early-morning sun blazing down on us was absolutely unbearable. Matteo, however, was as perky and talkative as ever, filling every moment of silence with stories and questions and whatever other thoughts popped into his head. I liked being in his company – even when I was hungover – and even though we'd never said anything about it out loud, we'd grown so attached to each other that it had started to feel like he was my secret boyfriend.

'Don't try to keep up with my friends next time,' he said with a laugh as I hopped off the back of his Vespa. 'Stay out of trouble today, okay?'

Matteo had some errands to run and so, for the first time, would be leaving me unattended with the students. It made me more nervous than it probably should've, and of course the kids instantly spotted my weakness and acted out accordingly.

'Where's Matteo?' Giovanni asked repeatedly, being as

deliberately loud and obnoxious as possible as he tossed balls of paper flirtatiously at the girls at the back of the room.

'He'll be back tomorrow,' I said, and immediately attempted to distract them with a simple love letter I'd written on the blackboard. I'd hoped to get them to write a letter to the fantasy partners we'd drawn the day before, but the kids weren't interested in the slightest. Giovanni had already grown bored of his bigbreasted fantasy lady and was now attempting to chat up every girl in the room. I couldn't fault his enthusiasm. He was a trier – I'll give him that – and he bounced back from every rejection he met with an idiotic amount of confidence.

'*Giovanni, che schifo!*' Ginevra winced as he whispered something into her ear. 'That's disgusting.'

'Back in your seat please, Giovanni,' I said for the third time, but he ignored me. He was utterly relentless that day. They all were, and they truly tried my patience right until the school bell screamed through my pounding headache at the end of the day.

'All right, go home, you monsters,' I told them with relief, squeezing the bridge of my nose as I sat back in my chair and waited for the classroom to clear.

'*Tutto bene?*' Giovanni called, stopping to lean against the doorframe as he made his way out of the room.

'In English?' I said. I wasn't supposed to speak Italian with my students, and that was one rule I didn't intend to break.

'You okay?' he repeated.

'I'm fine, thank you, Giovanni.' I smiled, looking up at him. He lingered for a few moments as if he wanted to say something, before turning on his heel and disappearing into the hallway. I obviously wasn't supposed to have favourites but I always had a soft spot for him. He was as troublesome as they come and a massive pain in the neck – I could hear him harassing his class-mates in the hallway even as I sat there – but he never failed to make me laugh and something told me there was a heart of gold underneath it all.

I waited for a few minutes as the cluster of noise disappeared from the corridor, and just as I was about to get up and head out myself, another face peered around the doorway. It was Caterina, the headmistress. She always wore her hair in a fiercely white Miranda Priestly bob, but she had a distinct kindness to her that was buried between the laugh lines left by forty years of doing a job that she loved. She seemed bemused by my flamboyant teach-ing methods, but would always smile with approval whenever she popped her head in to see how everything was going.

'How are things?' she said with a weak smile, her warm flame beginning to flicker as she made her way around and perched herself on the end of my desk.

'Things are good, why?' I asked, immediately suspicious.

'You know we support everything you do here,' she began, wringing her hands. 'But we've had a complaint, and I'm obliged to follow up.' She paused for a moment and let out a deep, exag-gerated sigh. 'Of course, the views of this particular parent don't reflect my own,' she began, 'but Giovanni's father would be more comfortable if we moved him to another class.'

'Another class?' I gulped, remembering his wildly inappropri-ate drawing of his fantasy girlfriend. His dad couldn't have seen it, though, as the drawings were safely locked away in my desk drawer. I hadn't even finished marking them yet.

'He's just not happy with you talking about your . . . personal life,' she continued.

'What do you mean?' I said, but we both knew very well what she meant. All of my fears over opening up about my sexuality were about to be realised. And it wasn't going to be me, but one of my students, who would be forced to pay the price.

'You were warned,' Caterina said. 'You knew this could happen. I just don't understand why you had to bring it up. You know what these parents can be like.'

It was Giuseppe's face that entered my mind when she said that. It had never occurred to me that the students would tell their parents, but word travels fast in a small town like this and all it takes is for one person to say something for news to spread like wildfire.

'Of course I support you – we all do,' Caterina continued. 'But you're not going to be able to teach him any more. Do you understand?' Her calm and diplomatic demeanour was frustrating. I wanted her to be an ally – to stand up for me, to scream her outrage and do something to right this wrong. But she didn't. She wasn't actually on my side; she was on the side of the parents, and she'd do anything to make them happy. They were the ones paying a small fortune for this school, after all.

'Calum?' she pushed. 'Do you understand?'

I nodded dejectedly. I had congratulated myself on a job well done for coming out to my students, but here I was, saying nothing and letting my superior sell them down the river. I knew I was contributing to the problem with my silence, but selfishly I also knew that if I kicked up a storm, it would only alert

Giuseppe to who I really was. And that thought frightened me more than anything else.

'Are you okay?' Matteo said, catching up with me in the hallway after I finally left the classroom. He could read me like a book, and always knew when something was wrong.

'Yeah, no, I'm fine,' I said, avoiding eye contact. The look on his face made it clear that he didn't believe me, and it didn't take long for him to coax the truth out of me.

'It'll be fine,' he said. He didn't seem overly worried, but both of us knew that Giovanni's father and Giuseppe were friends. Matteo tried to take my hand, as if to reassure me, but this time it was me who withdrew.

We left the school in silence, and although I wanted nothing more than to hop on the back of his Vespa and have him take me as far away from there as possible, I knew that I'd eventually have to face the parents. There was always a buzz of excitement in the air on a Friday afternoon and the parents usually hung around the school gates, chatting about their weekend plans and cornering the teachers to find out how their precious ones were doing. I usually enjoyed those conversations – I found it very telling to meet the parents of my students, as there's an awful lot you can learn about a person from the way they raise their kids – but I didn't want to talk to any of them that day.

I'd met Giovanni's father a couple of times. He was a big, intimidating man with a handshake so firm you could feel your bones cracking as he squeezed your hand in his. He didn't speak any English, and so I was grateful that our conversations were always short. Thankfully he wasn't there that day, but his wife – Giovanni's mother – waved me down instead. She was a small timid woman with a warm smile and a big heart, and as we chatted and she asked what we'd been doing in class that week, it was clear that she was blissfully unaware of everything that had happened. She had played no part in this at all.

One of the local nuns made her way into the schoolyard then, and that was mine and Matteo's cue to leave. Admittedly she was never anything but friendly, and she spent all of her time engaging and giving back to the community, but I was feeling guilty enough already; the last thing I needed was to feel judged by the Catholic Church as well.

'*Buonasera, sorella,*' I said, trying to avoid eye contact as we skulked past and made our way over to Matteo's scooter. I could tell that he felt as anxious as I did – he was more jittery than usual, and where he usually held such strong eye contact, he was now looking everywhere but at me. We didn't say anything as he switched on the Vespa's little engine, and as we rode on in silence, I wondered if he, too, was thinking about his father.

The wind whipped past us noisily as we whizzed through the countryside and all I could think about was how the family might react. My hands no longer rested comfortably on Matteo's hips but now clung onto his jacket instead, leaving plenty of space between us. There was no more hiding in plain sight now. We took the long way home but there was no point in delaying the inevitable. I swallowed hard as we finally pushed open the front door and stepped back into their family home.

'*Ciao bello!*' Lorenzo squealed excitedly, his tiny feet scrambling towards me. It was a greeting I had grown to love, and as I lifted him up into the air he giggled with pure delight.

'*Ciao!*' Ornella yelled from the kitchen, the smell of herbs and spices drifting towards me. Matteo headed into the kitchen and I timidly followed him. Giuseppe was already sat at the kitchen table and gave a wide smile as we came in.

'Come, sit.' Giuseppe gestured. I nervously sat down opposite him. Matteo squeezed in next to me, his leg pressing up against mine, and began cheerfully rattling off in Italian. I usually listened intently when they spoke like this, trying to pick out words and phrases and figure out what they were saying. But today, I wasn't listening; today, I just watched. Giuseppe's lips curled upwards into a smile as Matteo spoke, and then he broke into a hearty chuckle and shook his head with disbelief as he listened to whatever hilarious anecdote his son was telling him. I was nervous at first, but the longer I sat there, the more I realised that he probably didn't know. Word hadn't travelled fast enough to reach this little country family home.

I realised that Matteo had been missing from my classroom that day because he'd gone to spend time with his dad. Giuseppe had taken a few days off work and they'd gone to the coast together to catch fresh mussels, knowing that they were my favourite. Ornella had lovingly prepared them with chilli and salt and was piling them high onto the table in front of us. I knew this was their way of saying that I belonged.

Giuseppe poured out a carafe of sweet wine from one of the

local vineyards and put it down on the table before us. Italians had a habit of letting their food do the talking, and there was an unspoken rule that you didn't discriminate when it came to food. This is so important to Italians that there was a public outcry that summer when one of the country's most beloved pasta-makers stated, on national radio, that they would never include a homosexual family in their adverts, and that gay customers who didn't like that could go buy their pasta elsewhere. While a publicly homophobic comment like that might have normally slipped under the radar, this time the Italian people responded with a boycott. It didn't matter who you were or who you loved – you were always entitled to good food.

'You are a part of our family, yes?' Giuseppe asked as he tore off a piece of bread and dipped it into the spicy sauce. 'I am happy when my family is together,' he continued, chewing contentedly with his mouth open. 'And I am very happy that you are here.' It was the nicest thing he'd ever said to me, and I only hoped he'd remember these words when he inevitably found out the truth.

'To our English son,' Ornella said, raising a glass of red wine as she joined us at the table. 'You have made our children very happy.' She ruffled Lorenzo's hair as he screwed up his face.

We stayed at the dinner table for hours that night, and by the time we got up to go to bed, I had all but forgotten about what had happened earlier that day. All I could think about was collapsing into that single bed with Matteo and letting every-thing wash away to the sound of our beating hearts.

But Giuseppe had other ideas. When we pushed open the door to Matteo's bedroom, there wasn't just one bed waiting for us – there were two. The sofa bed from downstairs had been pushed into the far corner of the room.

Giuseppe had known all along.

'At least you get some space now,' Matteo said, glancing across at the second bed. He tried to compensate with an uncomfortable laugh.

'I guess.' I smiled weakly and sat on the hard, lumpy bed that awaited me.

'I didn't mind sharing, you know?' Matteo said quietly, closing the door behind us. His mouth twitched as he watched me, his jaw tightening.

'I didn't mind, either.' I pulled off my T-shirt and tossed it into the laundry basket. There was a moment of silence as I considered suggesting we share anyway, but that would be admitting my feelings out loud, and I knew that wasn't something he was ready for.

'Night, then,' Matteo said, tugging his jeans off.

'*Buonanotte*, Matteo,' I replied as he flicked off the light, plunging us into darkness.

Chapter Four

Lorenzo took one look at the sea and shook his head, puffing up his little face in defiance. There was no way he was getting in. He looked as ridiculous as he did adorable in his oversized, bright-orange armbands. Despite relentless coaxing from his brother, he was adamant that he wouldn't even dip his toe.

'What if I carry you?' Matteo said, kneeling down on the hot sand and offering his back. Lorenzo climbed aboard, giggling with pure delight as Matteo took slow steps towards the water. His laughter masked Lorenzo's shrill little shrieks as the gentle waves began to splash against his legs, and it didn't take long until it was as if the boy's fear of the water had never been there at all.

I loved watching them like this. It was clear that Matteo would go to the ends of the earth for his little brother, and it made me wonder what I had done to be so lucky to land in the laps of this beautiful family. I loved them all, even Giuseppe, and in that moment I truly felt like I never wanted to leave.

Matteo was only knee-deep in the water when Lorenzo insisted on being passed over to me – his 'other brother' – and so we took it in turns to carry him, splashing around along the shoreline. I could see Ornella watching us as Giuseppe dozed beside her, a placated smile on her lips. She gave us a little wave and returned to her book.

'You wanna try by yourself?' Matteo said after a few minutes. Lorenzo nodded his head, looking down into the water with excited curiosity as his brother set him down in the shallows. He immediately began splashing us, his ankles barely submerged in the water, and squealed with delight as Matteo started chasing him along the shore. Ornella peered over the top of her book from time to time, laughing to herself as she watched her three boys playing on the sand.

All that excitement eventually built up an appetite for gelato and Lorenzo went back to his parents, leaving Matteo and me free to swim out into the deep. I loved being alone with him, out there in the quiet of the sea, bobbing up and down in the water. We took turns diving below the surface and trying to pull one another under: he made an attempt on my swim-shorts a couple of times, and I'd respond by dunking his head beneath the surface, my fingers catching in his matted hair as he tried to pull himself free. There was always an innocent playfulness between us, and I longed for these moments even more now that we were in separate beds. No matter where we were or what we were doing, we always found an excuse to be close to one another, whether that was the innocent touch of our hands colliding over the dinner table or his hands sliding into my shorts beneath the waves.

46

I didn't want to admit it at the time, but having separate beds probably wasn't the worst thing. In all honesty, I don't think Matteo was ready to share a bed; he had to organise his thoughts and feelings first, and he couldn't do that with me sleeping two-and-a-half inches away. Our interactions some-how felt more meaningful too – on our first night we'd skipped the shy and awkward flirting by being put in a bed together, so sleeping apart gave us a chance to get to know each other all over again.

Giuseppe had watermelon granita waiting for us when we went back to shore. Ornella unpacked an elaborate spread of *insalata di riso* and left-over arancini as Lorenzo impatiently peered into the picnic basket. She slapped his hands away as he tried to reach for the dessert before he'd even touched the plate she'd made up for him. That Saturday was uninterrupted bliss, and it would have stayed that way if I hadn't gone home that evening and remembered the pile of unmarked homework wait-ing for me on the bed.

It wasn't the fact that I had work to do but the thing that work reminded me of that bothered me. And of course it was Giovanni's homework that sat at the top of the pile. I picked it up and turned it over in my hands, his beautifully cursive yet barely legible handwriting instantly recognisable. He'd written long, descriptive sentences, his English near perfect, and he'd scrawled Ginevra's name in the corner and surrounded it with a crooked love heart. It would be the last piece of his homework that I'd ever mark, and I wondered if he'd hate me for it, if he even knew why he was being forced to change classes. I really didn't like the idea of going back to my classroom on Monday morning without him there, but I hated the idea of being confronted by him even more.

'Is it okay if I come in?' Matteo peered around the doorframe, as if still unsure of our new boundaries.

'It's your room.' I shrugged and turned back to the piece of paper in my hands.

Matteo closed the door behind him and sat cross-legged on the bed in front of me. I set down the homework and looked up at him.

'Is everything okay?' he asked. I shrugged my shoulders. He looked down at the homework and sighed.

'You should fight it.'

'How?'

He didn't seem to have an answer. He shrugged and stared at me with those eyes that seemed forever encouraging.

'Gabriele and Gianmarco are coming over soon,' he finally said. 'Maybe they'll know what to do?' He could barely finish the sentence without laughing.

'*Pagliacci*,' I said with a laugh. Matteo gave me a little nod, putting his hand on my knee for a moment, as if – unnecessarily – apologetic for his inability to help.

'It's fine,' I said, touching his hand for a second. The sound of the doorbell caused us to quickly pull away from each other. It was Gabriele and Gianmarco. I could hear them making all the noise of a pair of wild dogs from the moment Ornella greeted them at the door. I heard her call after them as they clumsily bounded up the stairs, but they ignored her and pushed their way through the door into Matteo's bedroom without knocking. That's the kind of friendship you have when you've known someone your whole life – it was clear that they treated this house as if it were their own.

They'd planned to go up onto the rooftop to watch the shooting stars that night; the skies were perfectly clear, and the meteor shower was all anyone had talked about for days. They eagerly invited me to join them, saying something about it being my initiation into the group, before arguing about whether or not the four of us would even fit up there.

I could see why – the slanted roof of the house was just big enough for all of us to squeeze onto, and it could only be accessed by hopping across from one of the enormous overhanging trees in the garden. It was entirely unsafe but Giuseppe and Ornella didn't seem to mind; they just warned us that we'd better not let Lorenzo see us.

'That boy's imagination is wild enough without you boys giving him ideas. *Capito?*' Ornella said as we headed out of the kitchen into the back garden. 'Behave yourselves, boys,' she said, 'and enjoy the stars.'

I was the last one up and Gianmarco had to catch me as I climbed across and almost slipped. He made an idiotic joke about me coming onto him as I landed in his arms. They had come prepared with bottles of wine and cigarettes, and we passed them back and forth, taking long drags and swallowing down gulps of Frascati. I didn't usually smoke and neither did Matteo, but it was fun to feel like a rebellious teenager again.

We even played truth-or-dare, a game normally reserved for curious teenagers. I know a lot of people who can relate when I say that I kissed my first boy *and* my first girl playing that game.

Long before I'd even figured out my sexuality, it was an opportunity to experiment without judgement – a chance for boys to kiss boys and girls to kiss girls without first having to declare to the world that they were gay. Sexuality didn't matter. Anything goes in truth-or-dare.

'Truth,' Matteo said after a long pause with the three of us eyeing him impatiently. Gabriele strummed his fingers on his chin as he tried to think of something, but the question was already forming on Gianmarco's lips. He let the words linger as he asked Matteo if he'd ever thought about kissing another boy. The tension hung in the cool night air as he spoke, teasing us as we waited for the answer to a question I'd so desperately wanted to ask.

I half-expected Matteo to crumble under the pressure, but he didn't. He shrugged his shoulders. 'I've never done it, but, sure, I've thought about it. We all have.'

Gabriele immediately protested and began bragging about all the girls he'd kissed, but Gianmarco, on the other hand, admitted that he had, too. I wished I'd had a friend like him growing up – he was as straight as they come, but I'm pretty sure he'd long since figured out that his best friend might be gay, and his support was as subtle as it was patient.

Watching all of this play out reminded me of how much older than Matteo I was. I was treating him like one of my peers but in terms of our experiences, we were a lifetime apart. I'd come out to my parents, moved in with Tom, built a life with him and then watched it all fall apart. Matteo had never so much as kissed another boy. He'd never built up the courage to tell someone that he was gay. I felt a little guilty then, wondering if what we were doing was wrong, and if I was somehow putting an unnecessary amount of pressure on him before he was ready.

'Truth or dare?' Gianmarco finally said, turning to me with one of his bushy black eyebrows raised. I could already see where this was going. Gabriele may have been unaware of it, but it seemed that Gianmarco had planned all of this in advance.

'Dare,' I said, meeting his gaze and knowing exactly what he was going to say.

'Kiss Matteo,' he said, without missing a beat. I looked to Matteo for permission. He gave me a little unbothered shrug as Gabriele nudged me in the side. Trying not to seem either too eager or too disinterested, I leaned in and let my lips touch his. He tasted like sweet wine and cigarettes, but I pulled away awkwardly, having kissed him the way one might kiss their grandmother's cheek.

I felt a little guilty that, after all that waiting, his first kiss should be so uneventful. He didn't seem to mind – he just laughed his quirky laugh, wiping his mouth with feigned disgust. Gianmarco seemed awfully pleased with himself; it was clear he'd accomplished what he'd wanted. I instructed him to kiss Gabriele as my revenge, but that's when they called the game to a stop, insisting that we were too old to be playing it anyway.

I didn't argue – it gave Matteo and me the opportunity to move a little closer to each other, to let our hands quietly find each other's while Gianmarco and Gabriele pretended not to notice. I lay back on the cool slate of the roof with Matteo beside me, his head resting gently on my chest. My heart must have been deafening as it pounded in his ear and we stared up into the night sky and waited for the shooting stars that would never come. I closed my eyes to the world and let Gabriele and Gianmarco's voices fade away into the background.

Matteo eventually sat up to light another cigarette, and just as he was doing so a booming voice cut through the silence, startling Matteo so much that he jumped and accidentally burned my arm with the lit cigarette in his hand. It was his father, who had appeared in the back garden and started yelling something about the time. Matteo yelled back in Italian before turning to us, saying that we'd better get down.

'I'm sorry,' Matteo added, noticing me nursing the fresh cigarette burn on my arm as the four of us climbed back down from the roof. Gabriele and Gianmarco kissed me on both cheeks, then turned and followed Matteo as he led them back through the house to the front door.

Ornella had already taken Lorenzo up to bed, and as I headed through the house and into the kitchen, I found myself stood alone with Giuseppe. We were almost never alone together, and when we were it always reminded me of that silent drive on my first day here.

'Drink?' Giuseppe said. He was cradling a near-empty glass of wine, staring out of the window into the garden, his usually warm demeanour now decidedly more serious.

'No, thank you.' I leaned awkwardly on the kitchen counter.

'You know the neighbours see you up there?' he said in broken English, gesturing out of the window. He took a long and considered sip of his wine. I didn't know how to respond, and so I just stood there in silence, holding my breath and waiting for his next words.

'My son likes you very much,' he continued. 'But my son is just nineteen years old. He doesn't know what he wants.' He turned round to face me, and I was so taken aback by his honesty that all I could do was nod.

The words of the man I'd met on that first night seemed so at odds with the man who stood in front of me now. His ferocity now seemed extinguished, and all that remained was the small and unthreatening frame of a concerned father. He opened his mouth as if to speak again, but was interrupted by Matteo, who was now noisily coming through the front door after having bid farewell to his friends.

'Bed?' Matteo came over to join us and smiled. Giuseppe smiled back, covering over all traces of the conversation we'd just had.

'*Si, sono stanco*,' I answered, and they both laughed at my terrible pronunciation.

'Goodnight, Calum,' Giuseppe said, draining the final drops from his glass.

'*Buonanotte*, Giuseppe,' I said, and we quietly climbed the stairs up to bed.

Giovanni's desk sat empty in my classroom when I walked in the next day. Ginevra looked at it and sighed. She remained on her very best behaviour even though her classmates misbehaved right through the rest of the afternoon. It was clear that she knew what had happened.

'I'm sorry,' a small voice came from the hallway as I was tidying up the classroom at the end of the day. I turned round to see

Giovanni, a sheepish look on his face. It was a look that hit me deep in the gut. He came in, shuffling his feet, and sat at his old desk, burying his head in his hands as he did. I waited for a moment, letting the awkward silence consume me, before pulling up a chair next to him.

'You really miss this class that much?' I asked. He shook his head without looking up. 'At least you get a break from Ginevra,' I tried to joke, but he didn't respond. It killed me to see one of my students like that. I didn't know what to do or say.

'I'm really sorry, Giovanni.'

Giovanni lifted his head a little and looked at me. His eyes were full of fear, and as his hands began to tremble, he opened his mouth and said those few words I'd never thought I'd hear him say.

'I think I might be gay.'

'Oh.'

Even though I'd once been in this exact same position myself, I had no idea what else to say. Nobody had ever come out to me before, let alone one of my own students. 'Well, that's great,' I added, with a slightly hesitant smile. I wanted this to be a celebratory moment, and I wanted to mean those words so badly. All I could do was worry, though. About this town, about his father, about how difficult things could be.

I now understood why so many parents worry when their child comes out to them. It's difficult to be supportive when you learn that life suddenly has the potential to be so much harder, and it's almost understandable why some parents would try to wish away the gay, rather than see their child have to go up against a deeply intolerant world.

I couldn't believe I had spent so much time obsessing over Matteo's sexuality when Giovanni had been sitting in front of me all along. I thought back to his big-breasted fantasy girl-friend, and to how he'd so brazenly flirted with every girl in the room. It reminded me of myself when I was his age. It had all been for show.

'You can talk to me whenever you want,' I said, after another long silence.

'And when you're gone?' His voice was soft and croaky. We both knew that the end of summer school wasn't all that far away now.

'We'll stay in touch. We can email.' I wished it was enough, but I knew that it wasn't. He needed someone here. I badly wanted to tell him about Matteo, but knew it wasn't my place to out him.

'But first,' I continued, 'let's get you back into this class.'

Giuseppe excitedly ushered me into the house that evening, practically pulling me through the front door. He led me into the kitchen, where a large plastic container sat in the middle of the table, and marvelled as he pulled off the lid and asked me to peer inside.

It was a kilo of fresh buffalo mozzarella. To Giuseppe, it was worth its weight in gold.

'*Bellissimo*.' He kissed his fingers and retrieved a plate from one of the cupboards. 'You want to try?' he said, gently cutting off a piece and carefully displaying it before us on the table. We each took a fork and tried a small mouthful, the moistness of the thick creamy cheese making me salivate.

'*Mozzarella di bufala*.' Giuseppe beamed. 'The very best.'

'*Delizioso*,' I said. I meant it, but there must have been something in my voice that made him guess there was something else on my mind.

'You're sad.' It wasn't a question. 'Is it about my son? About Matteo?'

I shook my head, and he looked even more puzzled. I was hesitant; I knew there was only so much that I could tell him, and without outing Giovanni, it was difficult to explain why this meant so much to me.

'If there's anything I can do to help,' he said, his eyes open and earnest, as though he so badly wanted for me to trust him.

'It's about one of the boys in my class. Giovanni.'

'Francesco's boy?' It made me nervous to hear him refer to Giovanni's father by his first name. 'What about him?' He sat down at the table, gesturing for me to do the same.

It felt so strange to have this conversation here, back at the same table where he'd said those horrible words all those weeks ago.

'They've taken him out of my class. His dad, the school, they don't want me teaching him any more.'

'*Perchè*?' He took another piece of mozzarella.

I didn't need to answer. He sighed deeply as he figured it out for himself.

'I'll take care of it,' he finally said, after a few moments' thought.

'Take care of it how? I already spoke to Caterina, and—'

'I'll take care of it,' he said again, and stood up.

'Thank you, Giuseppe,' I said quietly, after a pause.

He gave a soft, approving grunt.

'Family take care of each other,' he added, and walked out of the room.

Giuseppe's acceptance of me wasn't something that had happened overnight. And even then, I could see his internal conflict tearing at him from the inside. A father figure standing up for his adopted son, even though it went against everything he'd ever known or understood. We didn't speak about Giovanni again, but after a couple of days he was back at his desk, as if nothing had happened at all. I wasn't exactly sure what Giuseppe had done or said, but I'm guessing he went to his father. I tried not to treat Giovanni any differently after that, but Matteo said it was abundantly clear that he was my favourite.

Whenever I tell people this story, they often find it remarkable that the gay kid just so happened to find himself in my class. But the truth is that there's a gay kid just like Giovanni in every single class and in every single school, and if we're unable to teach them that it's okay to be gay, then we probably shouldn't be teaching them at all.

I cancelled all lessons on the last day of summer school, and we went out onto the sports pitch to play one last game of capture-the-flag. I made Giovanni and Ginevra team captains, as they were easily the most athletic of the bunch, and when Giovanni insisted that Matteo be on his team, Ginevra insisted that I join hers too. I thought I'd have to go easy on them, but Matteo and Giovanni ran circles around me, high-fiving each other as they snatched our flag and ran it back to home base.

Ginevra waved her arms at me in frustration, then laughed as I struggled to catch my breath. 'You are an old man,' she said as she sprinted past me, tackled Matteo and then snatched back our flag.

Ginevra and I lost the game by an embarrassing amount, but seeing the joy on Matteo and Giovanni's faces as they claimed their win was sweeter than any victory could've been. They walked off the pitch together, arms wrapped around one another, and as they waved their flag in triumph I noticed a friendship already beginning to blossom.

Giovanni was the last kid I hugged goodbye at the end of that day. We took a group picture outside the front of the school, and when I waved them off I knew that I probably wouldn't see them again. Matteo came and found me in my classroom later, tidying up the last of the discarded books and pencils lying scattered around the room.

'We beat your ass today,' he said, and tossed a ball of paper at my head.

'I let you win.' I tried to reach down for the ball of paper, but as I did Matteo grabbed hold of me instead and pulled me into a hug. He wrapped the whole weight of his body around mine, and I let the books I was holding fall to the floor just so I could hug him back.

'What's wrong?' I said, feeling like my arms could have crushed him.

'I like you,' he said, his voice small and quiet, muffled by the weight of my body pressed against his. 'But I'm not gay. I like girls, too.'

It was the first time he'd said the words out loud, and they were full of so much raw and vulnerable honesty. I couldn't believe that he was the second person to come out to me within the walls of that classroom.

'Thank you for telling me.' My voice cracked under the weight of his words, because for all the compassion I felt for him in my heart, I knew there wasn't enough to carry him through the difficult days that would surely follow. He'd taken care of me every second I'd been here, and it was hard seeing him struggle like this.

'Maybe I'll tell my mom,' he said after a long silence. I nodded softly, squeezing him a little tighter as I felt his body tremble. I think Ornella had known all along. I had a feeling she'd figured it out long before I came here; she was just waiting for him to tell her.

I eventually tried to slowly pull away from the hug, but Matteo didn't let me. He held on to me while the school fell silent around us and, although we had another few days together, I realised that this was our goodbye.

It hadn't rained all summer, but the heat of Lucifer finally began to let up and relent, and we could hear the gentle pitter-patter on the grass outside as the sky began to fall.

I spent another few days with the family after the summer school shut its doors, and then knew it was time for me to leave. I felt at home here, but this wasn't my home. It wasn't where I belonged.

The family prepared a final feast for me on my last day. Even Lorenzo chipped in, helping to make the pasta with his teeny-tiny hands. Giuseppe clapped me on the back and referred to me as his son more frequently than usual; Ornella welled up whenever anyone mentioned that I was leaving, and Matteo unconvincingly acted as if he didn't care that I was going at all. I sat down opposite Giuseppe at the dinner table like I had on my first night, and he reached out and took one of my hands, beaming.

'I can't wait to have my room back,' Matteo joked as he slid into the seat next to me and took a slice of pizza from my plate. 'You've been cramping my style.'

'Is that right?' I said, one eyebrow raised. Matteo grinned.

All of them accompanied me to the train station after the meal. Lorenzo sat next to me in his car seat, refusing to let go of my arm the whole way, and Ornella kept saying that I'd be back one day, and that this wasn't goodbye for good.

She took both of my hands into hers while we were waiting for the train on the platform.

'*In bocca al lupo*,' she said. *Into the mouth of the wolf* – I now knew it meant good luck, and she said it with every ounce of her being as she struggled to hold back her tears.

'*Crepi il lupo*,' I responded, and she smiled encouragingly. *May the wolf die.*

'*Bravo*, Calum.' She slowly let go of my hands, pleased with all she'd taught me.

Giuseppe came in for a final hug. 'My English son.' He beamed.

'*Il mio papà Italiano*,' I answered. All of my fear and anxiety was gone, and I now trusted him as if he were my own father.

I never thought it would be so difficult to leave. I held Matteo for a little too long when I embraced him for the final time. It was all I could do in that Italian train station, surrounded by people. I wish I could tell you that we finally shared a kiss, but the only kiss we'd ever share would be in that game of truth-or-dare. I think we were both okay with that. Our story was never meant to be romantic – Matteo and I were friends, and we'd both find someone special as soon as we were ready.

I felt a lump forming in my throat when I finally boarded the train, but it was seeing Lorenzo burst into tears that finally broke me. I didn't know if I'd ever see any of them again, and of all the goodbyes I'd ever said, that would be one of the hardest.

I'd go on to teach in many other schools that summer, but none of my students or families would ever mean as much to me as they did. I vowed that I'd never lie about my sexuality again, and sure enough more students would eventually come out to me, just like Giovanni had. There would be more men like his father – men who were stuck in their ways – but there would also be men like Giuseppe, who were more than willing to change. He'd had his arm around Matteo when the train finally pulled out of the station, and it gave me hope that everything was going to be okay.

While it is of course normal for us to want to shut out those who don't first understand us, sometimes people can be surprising, and where it's safe and possible to do so, showing a little empathy and understanding can often be a much-needed catalyst for change. All it took for Giuseppe to open his mind and heart was for him to understand that we were just ordinary people like him.

Much as Giuseppe had changed his mind that summer, the Italian people in general were changing their minds too. The people who went on record to support same-sex marriage had always been a minority, but that number was growing rapidly, and less than two years later, for the first time ever, they would become the majority. A majority that would lead to the legalisation of same-sex unions in the country – an enormous step forward for people like Giovanni and Matteo, and for LGBT+ Italians everywhere.

GERMANY

Chapter Five

Neon lights flickered through the open window and cast shadows across our naked bodies as we lay on the lone inflatable mattress on the empty warehouse floor. Frank Ocean played quietly over a vinyl player next to us as a battery-powered fan whirred noisily in the background.

He was telling me one of his stories. I watched him intently, inhaling his words in the midnight air. His name was Jack. He had dark skin, deep-brown eyes and a lazy New York drawl that seemed to completely disappear whenever he spoke German in a near-perfect accent. He was the first guy I'd so much as gotten close to since Matteo, and while I hadn't known what would happen after Italy, I never expected that I'd end up following a complete stranger to Berlin.

I'd been working in the Alps when I met him. I'd got another job teaching in a Swiss summer school, and much like in Italy, I found myself once again living in the middle of nowhere. The rolling landscapes and exquisite sunsets went a long way towards making up for it, however; each night, the sky would come alive with wisps of pink and orange and the other teachers and I would sit around the campfire, watching the sun disappear between the snow-covered mountaintops. It was the perfect romantic destination, and many of the other teachers would take advantage of this, coupling up and feeding each other sticky-sweet marshmallows around the fire each night.

Nothing quite stirs up feelings of loneliness like being the last person around a campfire after everyone else has gone home. Sometimes it made me feel like I was the only gay man for miles. After all, the opportunities for a summer romance are significantly harder to come by when you're travelling as a gay man. I was envious of my peers – sometimes we'd head into the only bar in town to chat up the backpacking tourists that were passing through, but they were usually straight men with haggard beards and dreadlocks, or straight-out-of-college couples who were exploring on their gap year. The other teachers would take their pick of tourists and locals each night, but despite my best efforts, I would always go home alone. At least until I met Jack.

We'd just ordered a couple of bottles of wine to our candlelit table outside when he cockily came over to us. I didn't like him at first – hated him, in fact – as he was loud and assuming, and seemed just like your typical ladies' man. He flirted with the girls and carried himself arrogantly, demanding everyone's attention at all times. I rolled my eyes as he rattled through a string of offensive jokes.

'Do you like drinking games?' he said in his thick Brooklyn accent, turning his attentions to me as he slumped down without so much as introducing himself.

'I guess so,' I said dismissively, knowing we were going to play whether I wanted to or not. He smirked and got back on his feet, once again insisting that everybody pay attention to him while he explained his idiotic game. He had curly black hair, coarse stubble and a strong jawline, and despite my better judgement, something about him started to lure me in. His cockiness had somehow become increasingly charming, and although I tried really hard to be annoyed by him, I couldn't stop myself smiling as I listened to him explain the rules.

'So seven and fourteen are switched, and once you get to twenty one you pass your drink to the left.' He took my drink out of my hand and handed it to the girl next to me.

'Got it?' he asked, sitting down opposite me.

'Not even a little bit.' I laughed and he shook his head.

'You'll catch on.'

'What does your T-shirt say?' I asked, pointing to the black German lettering across the front of it. *Ich bin schwul, und das ist auch gut so.*

'I'm gay, and that's a good thing,' he answered with a little wink.

We played that game for what seemed like for ever. I still didn't understand the rules by the time we were finished, but if the objective was to get drunk then I was definitely winning. By the end of the evening everyone at our table had paired up and slunk off into the night, leaving me and Jack by ourselves.

'You gonna be all right getting back?' he said, helping me up onto my feet as I struggled to gain my balance.

'I'll be fine.' I smiled and then deliberately stumbled, letting him catch me.

He put his arm around me as we made our way down the street. My favourite thing about this little town was how prettily it twinkled in the moonlight. There were no streetlights, and so the locals hung lanterns outside their doorways or lit candles in their windows, almost as if to help guide drunken visitors safely back to their beds.

Jack's cocky attitude had begun to fade as he guided me through the winding streets to the little cottage he was staying in. It was so basic that the door didn't even have a lock, and the weak electric light hummed noisily as he pulled me through into the dimly lit hallway. It was a world away from the fancy hotel I'd been staying in.

He led me out onto a wooden balcony that creaked when we stepped onto it. It was tenuously suspended over the edge of the mountainside, and I could hear rocks from the cliff-face crumbling down into the roaring river that snaked through the valley below. The moonlight sparkled as it reflected off the water, and although it was impossible to see anything else in the pitch darkness, it was evident that in the full light of day the view must've been breathtaking.

'How did you find this place?'

'Google.' He shrugged. 'I just got here yesterday. I leave tomorrow. More wine?' He disappeared back into the kitchen and returned with a bottle of red and two glasses. I looked down as he poured out the wine, suddenly nervous about the rickety platform we were standing on, but he did his best to distract me with extravagant stories of his travels. He'd seemingly been everywhere and seemed free of responsibility – always on the road, always hooking up with guys and always looking for the next big adventure.

'Do you never miss home, though?' I asked, as I began to relax into the death-trap we were standing on. He took another sip of his wine and then silenced me with a slow and passionate kiss, spilling his wine as he grabbed me and pulled me closer. I think he wanted to have sex with me right there on the balcony, but I'm pretty sure even the smallest amount of vigorous movement would have sent us both to an early grave.

'Bedroom?' I said coyly, but he didn't stop kissing me, and so I started to manoeuvre him inside instead, carefully trying to put down our glasses as he tore at my clothes on our way to the bedroom. He seemed to pull my clothes off with ease, while my fumbling hands accidentally ripped his T-shirt and my fingers became useless as they tangled up in his belt buckle. I felt so inexperienced and out of practice, but he didn't seem to care. He laughed as he batted my hands away from his belt and unfastened it himself.

He stood up in front of me and stripped. He seemed so much smaller and more fragile without his clothes on – his arms were thin and his chest sunken – but he himself remained as confident as ever when he wrapped himself around me.

The sex was awkward and uncomfortable, but I enjoyed it all the same. I'd never been with an American guy before and had never seen a circumcised penis outside of porn, and I was almost embarrassed that I wasn't quite sure what to do with it. He, however, confidently told me that he'd been with dozens of uncut guys. It was a strangely intimate way to bond, trying to figure out a body foreign to me. I could feel myself warming up to him, starting to trust him and letting my guard down.

I felt incredibly safe and satisfied when I fell asleep in his arms that night, but the interesting thing about Jack was that I wasn't even sure if I fancied him. He certainly wasn't my usual type, but I found something about him alluring, something about him that pulled me in, deep.

'Where are you going next, then?' he asked me the following morning. We were sitting cross-legged on the end of his bed, watching the sun rise over the snow-topped Alps, bringing the world to life around us.

'I honestly have no idea. I'll figure it out,' I said, unconvincingly.

'Well, that's the best situation to be in.'

He gave a wicked smile, and grabbed my hand for just a moment before jumping up from the bed. He rummaged through his backpack and tossed me something.

It was a fold-out map of Europe.

'Here, take your pick.'

The map was worn and tattered. Various scrawls and squiggles had been written all over it. The little hilltop town we were staying in had been circled, and an arrow with a question mark had been drawn against it, leading straight to Berlin.

'It's a nice idea,' I began, 'but I'm not about to decide my future on a whim.'

'Your future?' He laughed. 'Who said anything about your future? We're just deciding on tomorrow. And the day after that. Tell me, where do you want to go?'

'I don't know,' I said, only half taking him seriously. There were so many places I'd never been, so many places I wanted to visit, but spontaneity didn't come naturally to me. I couldn't live my life like Jack did.

'What if we do this, then?' He took my hand in his and placed his other hand over my eyes and began running my finger along the map. 'Tell me when to stop.'

'Stop.' I laughed as he slammed my finger down on the map.

'Looks like you're going to Frankfurt, then,' he said, taking his hand away from my eyes. 'It's not too far from Berlin. That's where I'm headed; maybe you could visit after?'

I didn't know if his offer was sincere, but just getting up and going to Germany for no reason seemed a little more than reckless.

'I'll think about it.'

I did. I thought about it when we had sex again that morning, and again when he put his number into my phone after we kissed goodbye. I thought about it on the walk back to my hotel, and then every day at school when I showed up to teach. I had no idea where I was going to go next, and the idea of going to Germany on a whim seemed more and more appealing as the days went on. I finally gave in on my last day of work, booking a train ticket for myself and the cheapest room I could find.

It was probably the most spontaneous thing I'd ever done. Although I second-guessed myself the whole way, I knew deep down that it was absolutely the right decision to make. The truth is, I saw something in Jack that I aspired to – I'd played it safe my whole life, had never taken risks and had always made what everyone considered to be 'responsible' decisions. I'd met very few gay men who were like Jack, who seemed so sure of themselves and were so confident and decided in their actions. There was nothing about Frankfurt that particularly appealed to me and I didn't even know what was there, but I couldn't shake off a growing thirst for adventure. I wanted to be a little more reckless for once.

I wanted to be a little more like Jack.

It was late at night and pouring with rain when I finally arrived in Frankfurt. The train had been heavily delayed, I was tired from lugging my heavy suitcase and the fun of the spontaneous trip had already started to wear off. That's the thing people forget to tell you when they talk about their adventures on the road: they always give you the highlight reel, glossing over the miserable bits and forgetting to tell you how gruelling and lonely it can sometimes be. I knew the hotel was within walking distance of the station but my phone had no signal, and without a map of the city I soon found myself wandering through the red-light district, hopelessly lost and cursing Jack for making me come here.

Frankfurt's red-light district lies in an area known as Bahnhofsviertel just across the road from the train station, and is one of the biggest in the world. If I wasn't so eager to find my hotel I probably would've stopped to notice the silhouettes of naked women in the neon glow that beamed from every window, reflecting in the puddles on the wet tarmac.

'Are you okay?' a friendly voice called after me as I stopped dead in my tracks, yet again hopelessly checking my phone for signal. 'Do you need some help?'

I looked up and saw a tall woman smoking in one of the doorways, wearing a pair of bright-red stilettos and a revealing black leather outfit.

'I'm just a little lost,' I said with a hint of frustration. 'I'm trying to find my hotel. Maybe you know it?'

I gave her the address but she just took another long drag on her cigarette and shrugged.

'Don't know it,' she said, sympathetically. 'But maybe you'd like to come in? Catch a show? Get out of the rain?'

I looked up at the red 'XXX GIRLS GIRLS GIRLS' neon sign that flashed above the doorway, and shook my head a little awkwardly.

'Not really my thing.'

'Oh well, I could've guessed.' She laughed. 'Maybe you should try that way then? Find your people?'

She pointed to an alleyway across the street and I could just about make out a rainbow flag billowing in the distance.

'I really should just find my hotel.' I smiled, trying not to sound ungrateful.

'Christopher Street Day?' she said. I looked at her, a little confused. I had no idea what she was talking about. 'Just trust me. You'll find what you're here for.'

She tossed her cigarette onto the floor and stamped it out, giving me a little wink as she went back inside. I really was lost, but I figured that if I was going to be lost anyway, I might as well be lost among my own people. The rainbow flag was something I always looked for in a new city – no matter where in the world I found myself, I always knew I would be safe whenever I saw those colours.

I saw more and more of them as I made my way down the alleyway, and I could hear the familiar sound of throbbing club music getting closer. It was a Friday night, but even so it was far busier than I'd expected. The bars were so packed that people were piling out of them and into the street, and everyone seemed to be dressed in their best and most extravagant outfits, sparkling with glitter and rainbow paint, as they laughed loudly and huddled together to shelter themselves from the rain.

I looked around for somebody to ask directions from but everyone was speaking in a flourish of different languages, and it seemed like almost everyone was from out of town. I finally spotted a pair of nearly naked drag queens trying to hide their hair and make-up beneath a tiny umbrella. I knew that if anybody knew this city, it would be them.

They looked at me with confusion at first when I asked them for directions, but when they heard the name of the hotel they nodded enthusiastically and pointed towards the end of the street. I gave them my best '*Danke schön*' and they waved me off with a sweet '*Tschüss*' as I went. They sounded nothing like any of the stereotypes about the German language I'd been led to believe – I'd expected it to be harsh and aggressive, but instead I found it to be remarkably soft and gentle. Especially when it was coming from a pair of glammed-up drag queens.

It wasn't until I reached the end of the street and turned into an enormous, crowded square that I understood what my friend in the red-light district had been trying to tell me. A huge decorative screen stood in the centre of the square, the words CHRISTOPHER STREET DAY emblazoned across it.

Christopher Street Day, as it turned out, was what they called Pride in Germany, in memory of the riots that had started outside the Stonewall Inn on Christopher Street in New York City in 1969 – considered by many to be the day the modern

LGBT+-rights movement began. Ending up here by chance seemed remarkably fortuitous – especially after already having stumbled into Pride in Rome – and I imagined Jack smirking to himself, as if he'd planned this all along.

I knew that I couldn't let him down, and promised myself that I'd find my hotel, ditch my suitcase and throw myself into the heart of the rain-soaked celebrations. And that's when I saw it – just across the square, lit up in rainbow colours and swathed in decorative flags, was the hotel I'd been looking for. As if luck wasn't already shining on me, I'd quite literally booked the gayest hotel on the gayest night of the year, and I didn't even know that I'd done it.

I headed for the nearest convenience store, grabbed one of the few remaining Radlers from the shelf, paid for it and then quickly made my way to the hotel. The man on the counter was wearing a rainbow-striped pair of lederhosen, and beamed at me as he checked me in.

'The party isn't going anywhere,' he said with a chuckle, noticing my eager fidgeting as he handed over my room card. 'It's only 11 p.m.'

'No time to waste,' I replied cheerily, and headed for the stairs.

'*Schönen Tag*,' he called after me, but I was so excited that I barely even heard him.

I took the stairs two at a time and was practically tearing off my clothes as I pushed my way into the hotel room. I popped the cap on the Radler and took it into the shower with me, and within a matter of minutes I'd towelled off, dried my hair and slipped into something considerably less conservative. A mesh top and short shorts seemed entirely inappropriate for the weather, but it was Pride, and I was in the mood to be visibly queer. It was something I couldn't have done in Italy, something I'd rarely got the chance to do in my hometown, and something so many of us only get to do just once a year at Pride. Getting the chance to be our true authentic selves and doing it loudly and without apology is what Pride is all about – I'd have painted rainbows on my cheeks and doused myself in eco-friendly glitter if I could have.

My hair was still a mess but there wasn't another second to waste. I downed the remnants of my drink and let my legs carry me down the stairs and out into the heart of the festivities. The rain was still pouring – heavier now, in fact – but it wasn't remotely dampening anyone's spirits. People were laughing and cheering and, while I spotted a few anti-gay protestors in the crowd waving picket signs, everyone else was in such a good mood that nobody seemed to care. A pair of girls even stood in front of them and pulled each other into a long, drawn-out kiss, the sound of cheering around them drowning out the protestors entirely.

It was comforting to know that we were the majority here, and that nobody was going to hurt us. That's the thing I love most about the LGBT+ community. We aren't without our drama, of course – we squabble, we argue, and we sometimes fight over boys, but no matter what, we know we always have each other's backs. It's a constant reassurance to know this every time I attend a Pride event, to know that if anyone tries to cause trouble, the strangers around me would rally to my side without a second thought.

I didn't really talk to anyone at first, but mostly just immersed myself into the crowd and let myself be taken in by it all. I felt particularly touched when I spotted a couple of parents with their teenage son; he had rainbow patches stitched into his jacket, and they were each holding a small Pride flag that they waved in tireless and continuous support.

People smiled in my direction as I meandered through the square, and the feeling of community was most noticeably felt when the crowd began to hush around me and I looked up to see black-and-white pictures of loved ones who had been lost appearing on the screen. It was a tribute to all those lost to HIV/AIDS, and although it started with just a few people singing quietly on the stage, the song rang out across the square, and soon the entire crowd was singing in unison. A stranger took my hand and the crowd became one as we let the lyrics and the moment wash over us. I think it was in that moment that I truly fell in love with my community.

Many consider Pride to be a party, and others a time for remembrance. Some see it as a protest, or a time to reflect upon the progress that we've made. But to me, Pride is all of these things, and that's what makes it so special. A time to raise a glass with good friends, to remember those who've come before us, to fight for the rights we haven't yet won, and to celebrate those we have. Pride is a chance for us to come together, and for so many LGBT+ people, it's the time for them to remember that they are valid, that they are loved, and that they are part of something so much bigger than those who may have turned their backs on them.

Just an hour earlier I had been wandering the streets, lost and alone, and now here I was, feeling more welcomed than I could remember. I thought about Giovanni and Matteo, and hoped that they, too, could one day experience this, to know that they will always have a family here, and that there truly is a place where they belong.

It was Matteo I was thinking about when a smiling face caught my attention. He seemed to be around the same age, was impossibly cute, and something in his smile was identical to Matteo's. He tried to pull me into conversation and, although I couldn't understand him, I was instantly enamoured with his sweet and delicate way of speaking.

I fumbled a few words from my secondary-school German classes but he just looked at me blankly, shaking his head. We decided to stick with one another anyway, doing everything we could to string together some semblance of a conversation. He had piercing blue eyes and bouncy blond hair that was matted by the rain, but I was mostly intrigued by the fact that he was wearing his right arm in a cast.

'Rugby,' he said with a bashful smile – thankfully, a word that was the same in both languages. His name was Florian, that much I understood; and he might've been from out of town, but even that I couldn't be sure of. He eventually took me by the hand and led me over towards a pop-up cocktail bar, pulling me under the canopy to get me out of the rain. We knocked back drink after drink and laughed uncontrollably as we tried and failed to teach each other our respective languages. I'd spent the past few months working as an English teacher, and yet I was still completely thwarted by this charming German boy and his devilishly good looks. Part of me definitely enjoyed the language barrier – I quite liked the anonymity of it – and knowing I'd probably never see him again gave me the freedom to be a version of myself that I hadn't yet met. I'd been defined by the same personality my whole life, but this was a chance to be someone different. Florian had no preconceived ideas about who I was, and so that night I could be anyone I wanted.

The boy pulled me back into the crowd to dance, the rain soaking our clothes as we pushed our wet bodies together and clumsily met each other's lips. He tasted like the passionfruit from the pornstar martinis, and the scent of the perfume he'd splashed on his neck was intoxicating.

We danced until the early hours of the morning, and as the music came to a stop and the crowds began to disperse, he put his hands around my waist and pulled me in so his crotch was pressed firmly against mine.

'Hotel?' he asked. Finally, something we could both understand.

I took him firmly by the wrist and guided him through the crowd to my hotel. It was convenient being so close, and we were giddy as we pushed through the double doors into the foyer. The guy in rainbow lederhosen was still working the night shift, and I could see him smirking as he watched us slink our way up the stairs.

As soon as the door was shut behind us we were on one another, tearing at each other's clothes and pushing one other around the room. It was as if he was imitating the kind of aggressive sex that you often see in movies or in porn, asserting his dominance as he pinned me up against the wall. His broken arm and small frame didn't hold him back, and as he pushed me into the bathroom, he bit down on my neck and whispered hot, sticky words into my ear.

He lifted me up onto the sink and clawed at my skin, pulling my legs around his body as he slammed me against the mirror. The taps dug into my back as he fucked me but I really didn't care. I wanted every single part of him.

He finally pulled me over to the bed to finish and collapsed down on top of me, dripping with sweat as he tried to catch his breath. I ran my fingers through his hair as he lay there, and, with small talk impossible, we had nothing left to do but sleep.

I never expected him to stick around, and sure enough he was gone when I woke up the next day. It took me a moment to remember where I was, and when I couldn't find my phone or wallet I was convinced that he had stolen them. He hadn't: my wallet was in the hallway and my phone was on the bathroom floor, both casualties of the night before.

My head was pounding as I lay back in bed, but all I wanted to do was text Jack and tell him what had happened. I desperately wanted to tell him about my spontaneous adventure, about Pride, and Florian, and the bruises on my back. I knew that he wouldn't be impressed by this, though; this was just another Friday night for him, another trip for the scrapbook, another notch on his bedpost.

I was just about to set my phone down and go back to sleep when a message pinged through. It was from Florian. There were just three words:

Love the world.

I guessed that he probably meant something like 'enjoy your travels,' or 'have a safe trip,' but somehow he'd sent something infinitely more poetic.

Love the world. 'I will,' I thought, as I read the words over and over in my mind.

I sat for a few minutes before I eventually gave in and wrote a message to Jack.

Your offer still stand? Do you still want me to come?

He replied almost instantly:

Yeah.

It was such a Jack way to respond. I wrote back:

On my way then

And with that, I was on the next train to Berlin.

Chapter Six

Berlin couldn't have been any more different from Italy. In Italy my sexuality had been something to be ashamed of, to keep secret; but here, my sexuality made me no different from anyone else. Berlin was full of people looking to break the rules; some were pierced and modified, and others had their hair sprayed brighter than the graffiti that decorated the concrete walls. The city was made up of wide streets, vintage clothes and good-quality beer, and it had a sense of openness that made me feel welcome from the moment I stepped off the train.

Jack knew Berlin like the back of his hand, and I think he took great pleasure in watching me get drawn in by it all. He had first come to visit the city with his parents not long after the fall of the Berlin Wall, and although he had just been a few years old then, he told me that he remembered it like it was a vintage post-card or a forgotten roll of film. He hated taking me to tourist attractions, describing them as 'a soul-sucking waste of energy', but delighted in taking me to coffee shops and flea markets in the less-visited parts of town.

Jack was thrifty, and he managed to get by with very little at all. He had a German passport from his mother's side of the family, and he used it to take up jobs all over Europe. He'd been a bartender, a receptionist and even a teacher like me, but he was currently out of work, and so he spent very little on food in order to have more to spend on beer. He would sometimes visit the local squatters' commune, or *VoKü* – short for *VolxKüche*, 'the people's kitchen' – a concept where squats opened their doors to the public to offer food, music and drink. Five euros could get you a decent meal, a couple of beers and a whole night of entertainment. It was just one of the many things that made Berlin unique.

Occasionally I'd persuade Jack to take me into the heart of the city, and he'd roll his eyes and call me a tourist as I'd rush towards one of the food stalls to purchase some overpriced currywurst. The warm peppery flavour was worth it, even if I had to listen to Jack lecture me about how shockingly uncool I was. We couldn't have been more different, but the days flew by rapidly when we were together, quickly turning to weeks; and before I knew it, I started to feel like I was actually living there.

Although we'd had such a sexually charged introduction, the strange thing was that Jack and I had not had sex – or even kissed – since I got to Berlin. We'd sleep in the nude and spoon one another in the cold of night, but we were arguably nothing more than friends. Jack would often go out and meet boys – his sex drive was insatiable, but Berlin had more than enough titillation to satisfy his libido. He would frequently disappear at a moment's notice for a Grindr hook-up, or to meet a 'friend from out of town'. I was continually fascinated by his ability to find sex anywhere and everywhere we went – he once excused himself from dinner to go to the bathroom and came back twenty minutes later to tell me he'd had a three-way in the alley out back. Jack's stories were always entertaining, even if I sometimes couldn't help questioning how many of them were actually true.

'Maybe we should decorate?' Jack joked as we awoke one afternoon in early autumn, climbing up from the deflating mattress and looking around the empty room. Almost a month had passed since I got here. 'A lick of paint, a few pictures, maybe somewhere to sit?' He gestured into the echoing space around him with a wiry smirk across his face.

There was a stack of dusty boxes piled in one corner but otherwise the space was completely empty. Its simplicity reminded me of that apartment I'd shared with Tom, and that familiarity made me feel like I was home. Nothing but exposed brick and wooden floorboards and light bulbs strung up with shoddy wiring that didn't look safe. Apparently one of his friends owned the place and was in the process of converting it into apartments. Jack had told me he was doing them a favour by living here and keeping out squatters, but somehow I didn't think that was true.

'It really is the greatest city in the world,' Jack said to me as we took a stroll through one of the quieter neighbourhoods of the city later that evening. The sun was starting to set and was casting corridors of warm orange light between the gaps of asphalt and concrete. I didn't know where he was taking me but he'd said there was something he wanted to show me. Jack had a limitless passion for Berlin, and loved nothing more than teaching me about the city. He showed me small details I'd otherwise never have noticed, and frequently told me that I needed to stop 'walking around with my eyes closed'.

'We have to remember our history,' he said, tapping the pink triangle stitched into his ripped denim jacket. Born from the same symbol LGBT+ people had been branded with during the Holocaust, it had become a modern-day symbol of queer resistance. 'Everyone knows about the awful things that happened here – the eradication of queer people and Jews and anyone that was different – but nobody ever talks about the uprising that happened long before that.'

We stopped on a street corner across from a supermarket. 'Right there,' he said, pointing at the unremarkable storefront. 'That's where it all started.'

'*Speisekammer im Eldorado*,' I read aloud from the sign. It was a supermarket that specialised in organic produce and health food. 'I don't understand what I'm looking at.'

'The Eldorado Night Club.' He held out his arms, presenting the supermarket in front of us. 'You're standing in the world's first gay village. There were around a hundred LGBT+ bars here in the 1920s, but this one was the most popular. It didn't matter if you were trans, gay or lesbian; everyone was welcome here.'

'But wasn't it illegal then?'

''Course it was. Didn't stop them, though – people were as loud and proud here as they've ever been. They tried to decriminalise homosexuality then, and they very nearly succeeded.'

'So what happened?' I asked, staring across at the empty supermarket.

'Fascism,' Jack replied. 'The Nazis came into power and quashed the queer rebellion. They closed the Eldorado in '33, and you know what happened after that.'

It was hard to imagine that all of this could've happened on this quiet and peaceful little street, and if it wasn't for people like Jack keeping its memory alive I could see how such an important part of queer history could've easily been forgotten. Jack led me across the street and into the supermarket and showed me a collection of black-and-white photographs displayed just inside. Pictures of the Eldorado in all its heyday glory, with drag queens and gay couples and cabaret stars to boot. It looked like a truly magical time and there was no sign of the terrible things that would happen next. There was just one photo that served as a reminder of that, and it's still etched into my mind to this day.

The boarded-up windows. The swastikas.

The soldiers and their rifles.

'This city is built upon the determination to never let this happen again. We live our lives openly and honestly for the people who had theirs taken away from them,' Jack said, interrupting my thoughts. He reached down and unbuttoned his jacket.

'*Ich bin schwul, und das ist auch gut so,*' he said, reading out the words on the front of his T-shirt. It was the same one he'd been wearing on the night we met. '*I'm gay and that's a good thing.*' These were the words, Jack told me, that Klaus Wowereit, then Berlin's mayor, had said in 2001 after coming out as gay during his election campaign.

'He believed in championing the rights of women, religious minorities and the LGBT+ community, and that's why people had voted for him. Because it doesn't matter who you are, or where you're from. Everyone is welcome in Berlin.'

* * *

86

'We're going out,' Jack said later that night as he finished making pasta in our makeshift kitchen. We used an electric hotplate to boil water and cook pasta, and that was essentially all we ate. He pulled up a wooden crate and sat down, lighting a tealight candle in the centre of the plastic garden table we were using as a dining table. He pushed a bowl towards me.

It was already past 11 p.m. Jack very much liked to stick to his own schedule: 'Eat when you're hungry, not when your watch tells you to,' he liked to say. Mealtimes with him couldn't have been any more different from mealtimes in Italy. There they had been the most important part of the day – we'd sit and eat an abundance of incredible food for hours – but here, food was just sustenance, something to fuel the night ahead.

'Where are we going?' I asked, taking a bite of the bland pasta pesto.

'It's a surprise.' He grinned. 'Wear whatever you want.'

'Yeah, but fancy, casual – how should I dress?'

'It doesn't matter.' He shrugged, wolfing down the pasta from his bowl. The clubs Jack liked to take me to usually had strict and often incomprehensible door policies: 'Wear black if you want to get in this place.' 'Cover up.' 'Be more slutty!' 'No, you can't wear that,' he would say. One evening he told me I looked too preppy and ripped the sleeves off my T-shirt. Sometimes I suspected he just liked telling me what to do.

'*Gespritzter?*' Jack offered, shaking an almost-empty bottle of wine, the remnants splashing around the bottom. It was common to mix wine with sparkling water on a hot day in Germany, and that particularly appealed to Jack's thrifty nature. Especially considering that we didn't have nearly enough for two drinks.

I finished my pasta and took my drink into the bathroom with me. I took off my clothes, stepped into the shower and let the luke-warm water wash over me. The bathroom door didn't close properly but I didn't really mind; Jack and I had got so comfortable with one another that privacy wasn't really an issue any more.

My stomach growled from the alcohol I'd put in the previous three nights as I took another sip of my spritzer. One more night wouldn't hurt, I told myself, knowing full well that I was lying. I threw on my clothes – jeans and a T-shirt, since Jack said it didn't matter – and when I was ready, followed him down the rickety spiral staircase and into the corridor below. The apartment didn't have an entryway of its own, so we had to walk right through the middle of a Chinese restaurant just to get in and out of the building. The two owners didn't seem to mind, and always greeted us with big welcoming smiles when we passed through, sometimes even sending up left-over food at the end of the night.

It was a long walk to wherever we were going. Jack hated public transport, and so we walked absolutely everywhere. What I liked about being out in public with him was that he had no qualms about hiding his sexuality – he'd always link my arm or hold my hand, and it was the first time another male friend had really done that with me. It's one of the things I've come to love most about my friendships with queer men. Free of any outdated notions of masculinity, we often openly express our affections for one another without fear of judgement, or of being perceived as somehow less masculine. I'd make many more friends like him over the years, but Jack would always be the first.

Chapter Seven

'This way, I think.'

We'd been walking for a solid half-hour but I still had no idea where he was taking me. The long corridors of Berlin's streets had started to merge and look the same. We eventually came to a stop beside a narrow and secluded passage, a single street lamp leaning over us, illuminating our faces and casting shadows into the alley.

'At least, I think it's down here,' he said, scratching his head with a puzzled expression. 'I've only been here once before.' He furrowed his brow as he scanned the street. 'Yeah, I'm pretty sure it's this way.'

We walked a little slower now as we made our way through the alleyway. A kitchen porter appeared in one of the doorways and emptied waste into the bins.

'*Guten Abend*,' Jack said nonchalantly, smiling, as we pushed by.

'*Guten Abend*,' the man replied plainly. We slipped past and took a left into another narrow and even more secluded passageway.

'Are you sure this is the right way?' I asked, but he ignored me, headed for an unmarked door and started trying to prise it open.

'It's one of these doors,' he said, trying another. I was convinced we shouldn't be doing this, but on his third attempt, a door creaked open and gave way to the sound of muffled dance music playing from somewhere deep inside.

'After you.' He smiled widely. With my intrigue getting the better of me, I went into the dimly lit entryway and headed down a flight of concrete stairs.

'And we're definitely allowed to be down here?' I asked, but he hushed me and waved me away. The sound of music intensified as he pushed past me on the stairway and pulled open a second door. Lights and music blasted from behind a lacy curtain that obstructed our view, and a member of staff sat smiling on a stool in front of it. They were bald and heavily modified, dressed in a harness and leather, and had an eagle tattoo covering their neck and part of their face.

'Just the two of you?' they asked in English, instantly recognising us to be foreigners.

'*Ja genau, zwei, bitte,*' Jack confirmed with a nod.

'And you've been here before?' They raised an eyebrow, as if to suggest that we looked a little out of place. Try as I might to blend in, I seemed to stick out wherever Jack took me. I opened my mouth to tell them that it was my first time but Jack interrupted me, loudly asserting that we were both regulars. I smiled nervously, now complicit in his lie.

'Okay, thirty for the two of you.' They smiled, and Jack paid them without a second thought. They took the money and handed us each a numbered canvas bag. I didn't know what it was for but I tried to act casual.

'I'm so confused,' I whispered to Jack. He shushed me and kneeled down to untie his shoes, and that's when I understood why he'd earlier told me it didn't matter what I was wearing. It was because we wouldn't be wearing very much at all.

Jack pulled off his jacket and T-shirt, kicked off his shoes and began unbuckling his belt. Not wanting to seem like the outsider or the newbie, I copied him without question, stripping down and putting my clothes into the bag until I was wearing nothing but my underwear. The person on the desk wrote the numbers from our bags onto our chests with a glow-in-the-dark marker and then pulled open the curtain for us to go inside.

'You could've told me to wear my good underwear,' I whispered as we pushed through the curtain and into the party. Jack was wearing his best jockstrap, and I was in a faded pair of black and white briefs.

'Well, you can take them off if you want.' Jack smirked, and as I looked around I realised that half the people in there had already done just that. It appeared to be a men-only space, but I don't think I'd ever seen such a diverse and eclectic group of men. There were guys not a day over twenty-one, and guys in their sixties; there were skinny guys, larger guys, and guys who looked like they'd spent their whole life in the gym. Some wore leather pup masks, others wore harnesses, and a few wore leashes round their necks as they were guided around the room by their dominant partners.

The room was decked out with large TV screens playing all kinds of hardcore porn, while go-go boys wearing nothing but jockstraps and pig masks danced in large cages suspended from the ceiling.

'I'm going to go check out the darkroom,' Jack said as I was taking everything in, giving my arm a squeeze before disappearing into the crowd of heaving bodies. Jack loved taking me out of my comfort zone, throwing me into the deep end and then leaving me alone to flounder. I thought about following him, but knew that he'd probably be hooking up with someone within minutes, and so I looked around the room for a friendly face instead. The most remarkable thing about the people in the room was how very unremarkable they were, once you got past the fact that everyone was naked or wearing some kind of fetish gear; they seemed like the most ordinary people you'd ever meet. And that's probably because they were – accountants and bankers, shop assistants and teachers, or people like me and Jack. We were just ordinary people who were happy to embrace their sexuality for the night.

A few people smiled in my direction but it was one of the bartenders who caught my attention first. I was clearly a fish out of water and he was watching me with amusement. I couldn't tell if he was naked or just shirtless, and I couldn't help peering over the bar to find out as he beckoned me over to join him. He was wearing nothing but a tiny loincloth-like apron that failed to conceal anything.

'First time?' he said, a smirk still stapled to his lips.

'Is it that obvious?' I laughed, having no reason to continue with Jack's lie.

'We don't get many tourists in here,' he said. 'It's a little over-whelming, but you get used to it pretty quick. What can I get you?'

'Tequila orange,' I said, and then stopped him as I reached for my wallet and realised I'd left it in my jeans. 'Where do people keep their money?' I scanned the naked bodies around the room. Not one of them had pockets.

'Right there.' He pointed to the number on my chest. 'You can pay when you leave,' he added, and began mixing my drink. 'But first one's on the house. Double tequila orange, right?'

'*Ja, danke*,' I said, taking a sip of what tasted more like a triple. 'Do you not mind having to dress like that?'

'It's not a uniform.' He laughed. 'I dress like this because I want to. The tips are better, for sure, but we can wear whatever we like.'

'Well it's a good look on you,' I said. He smiled and shook his hips.

'Go for a look around. My name's Tobi if you need anything.'

The place was built like a maze. It was a whole other world, and I was completely new to all of it. I followed a corridor lit in neon pink and found myself in a small padded cinema room where a vintage porn film, complete with aviators and handle-bar moustaches, was playing on the screen. The floor was cushioned, and although the room was big enough to fit at least twenty to thirty people, there was just a single pair of guys lying on top of one another, kissing each other passion-ately. There was something quite romantic about it; I might have completely misjudged the situation, but they didn't look like they were here for a one-night hook-up. They looked very much like they were in love.

'Want to join us?' one of them asked, looking up as they noticed me lingering in the doorway. He was a little older than me, toned but not muscly, with messy blond hair, dimples and a soft German accent that rolled off his lips. His partner was like a clone of him – same hair, same build, same piercing blue eyes that stood out against the backdrop of the rolling cinema screen. They were both wearing briefs – white Calvins – and their attentions were now solely fixated on me.

'It's okay if you don't want to,' he said with a smile, his hand running through his partner's hair, down his chest, and catching in the waistband of his underwear. It made a snapping sound as he playfully tugged and pulled at it.

'No, I do, it's just . . .' I hesitated, trying to think of an excuse. I thought of Jack in the darkroom – this is why he had brought me here. 'Yeah, okay, fuck it.'

I made my way over to join them, their hands reaching out for mine. They caught me as I fell forward into them, their soft lips immediately against my skin. 'I'm Calum.'

'I'm Lucas,' one of the boys said as he kissed me. 'And this is Oscar. He doesn't speak a lot of English.' He ruffled his partner's hair.

Trust and communication. It was evident that was what made their relationship work. They seemed to have a clear understanding of one another's boundaries and there was constant communication between them. Lucas looked into Oscar's eyes as he pushed his thumbs into his waistband, and Oscar gave him a little nod, as if telling him that it was okay to pull off his briefs. They didn't push or pressure each other, and they treated me in exactly the same way, moving at a pace I was comfortable with and being as tender and gentle with me as they were with each other.

It was so at odds with any of the negative assumptions I'd made about what a sex club was really like, and it was an enormous relief to see them taking my consent seriously. When I eventually decided I wanted to stop, the boys let me up without question. I would have happily spent the whole night with them, but I didn't feel like I was ready to have sex out there in the open for all to see just yet. So I told them I might come back later.

'See you later then,' Lucas said.

'*Tschüss*,' Oscar said sweetly and I slipped back out of the room.

I explored for a little while longer after that, stumbling upon a BDSM room built like a torture chamber, a room with wall-to-wall glory holes, and lots of little hideaways and love nests for people to tuck themselves away into. I found it all so fascinating: I'd heard stories about such places before and seen videos of them in porn, but it was exhilarating to experience it for myself. I thought about my hometown with its tiny little gay bar and how something like this had seemed so far out of the realms of possibility then. It had only been a few months since I'd left that world behind, and I almost had to pinch myself to remind me that this was all real – that I was actually here in Berlin, in some underground club I didn't even know the name of.

I pushed my way through a set of heavy wooden doors, excited to find out what lay within; but, I soon realised, it was just the bathroom. Two doors stood in front of me: '*Herren*' and '*Damen*'. I tried to remember which was which, and wondered why a men-only sex club would have a women's bathroom in the first place.

'They're both men's,' a familiar voice said from behind me as a sweaty arm wrapped around my chest. It was Jack. He smelled like sex and was dripping with sweat. 'They have to have a women's bathroom – legal requirement or something.' He reached for the door marked *Herren* and pulled it open. 'You coming?'

I always find the bathroom to be the thriving, beating heart of any gay club – it's where people go to talk and socialise, to escape the music and chaos outside. It's my favourite place in a club and this one was no different. It was enormous – big enough to house a dance floor of its own – and filled with dozens of guys who stood around in their underwear, fixing their hair or adjusting their harnesses as they chatted in a mix of different languages. They were mostly speaking German, a little bit of English, with smatterings of Italian and Spanish and other languages too.

A true metropolis that you wouldn't even know was there.

At first I felt a little like I was invading their space, being there as an outsider, like a tourist in a place that wasn't meant for me; but they were all friendly and greeted us with a smile as we walked in. I don't know what I had been expecting – perhaps something from a Frankie Goes To Hollywood music video – but, surprisingly, my entire experience was considerably more *relaxed*. The issue, I think, is that positive portrayals of these spaces tend to be almost non-existent, and that led me to grow up believing that they were somehow something to be afraid of. My experience that night, however – and indeed the many experiences that would come in the years that followed – showed me that they could be some of the most inclusive and inviting spaces in the world.

The fact that so many guys of all ages and body types felt free to show off their bodies without judgement was testament to that. Body shaming can be an enormous problem in the gay community, and it was refreshing – at least that night – to see that people were being kind and complimentary and treating each other with respect.

'There's people having sex under there,' Jack told me as he pointed to an enormous grate built into the centre of the floor. A group of guys were huddled around it. I noticed a few urinals lined up against the back wall, but nobody seemed to be using them.

'There's a darkroom directly beneath,' he said with a devilish smirk, and was already taking his dick out of his underwear as he made his way towards it. I couldn't figure out whether it was an act of sadism or kindness to use the grate, but I decided to try to join in anyway, standing next to Jack, who was clearly enjoying himself as he playfully crossed swords with the guy standing next to him.

I could just about make out the moving bodies in the darkness below. I tried my best but my bladder refused to cooperate, and I shied away to use one of the urinals instead.

'Couldn't do it?' Jack teased me afterwards as he joined me by the sink to wash his hands. 'Don't worry; I couldn't my first time either.'

It was a rare token of vulnerability. He didn't like to ever admit that he was flawed or anything less than perfect, and he would absolutely never admit that he was wrong.

'Want to go in the darkroom?' he asked, reaching into his jockstrap to readjust his bulge, plumping himself up as if to make himself look bigger than he actually was.

'That one?' I nodded towards the grate with a little apprehension.

'Not my kind of thing,' he said, shaking his head. 'I'll take you to a better one.'

There was a bowl of condoms and lube by the sinks, and so I slipped some into my underwear just in case, and was relieved to see Jack do the same. I sometimes wondered about whether or not he was protecting himself; these were the days before PrEP, or pre-exposure prophylaxis, a preventative treatment now commonly used to protect against HIV infection, and although I had no issue with Jack's active sex life, I often worried about him taking unnecessary risks. He'd told me that he'd had unprotected sex on more than one occasion, and it bothered me how unconcerned he seemed.

The darkroom was pitch-black. There was a glimpse of movement among the shadows as we entered, but everything disappeared again as the door shut behind us. I fumbled for Jack's hand as he guided me through the room, my eyes slowly starting to adjust.

I could see that the whole interior of the darkroom had been set out like a labyrinth. The room probably wasn't all that big, but the darkness made it seem infinite. It reminded me of those hedge mazes I loved to get lost in as a kid, except this time I could barely see where I was going, and I could hear the very adult groans of pleasure escaping from the walls around me. Every now and then we'd stumble upon people in the shadows – some alone, some in twos, others in groups of three or four.

Nobody spoke – they communicated with small gestures and glances. A gentle touch of the arm could be considered a proposition, and a polite shake of the head an outright refusal. It was important to understand the nuance of body language in a space like this; I immediately felt more vulnerable just by being there, and it was comforting to know that there was a code of conduct that allowed for my personal boundaries to be respected.

I could barely make out people's faces and I found the anonymity of it fascinating. I didn't yet want to have sex with someone without first knowing who they were, but I knew that was the ultimate fantasy for Jack. He loved to be the mysterious stranger, and so it was no surprise to me that he would be drawn to a place like this.

'I think I'm ready to leave,' I eventually said as we took another turn and descended into the deeper recesses of the maze. Jack loved pushing me out of my comfort zone, and although I usually obliged, I think I'd finally found where my limits were.

The sex here was noticeably rougher and more emotionally detached than what I was used to, and although I'd learn with time that some of the most enjoyable and rewarding sex could come from encounters just like these, right then and there in that moment, I felt incredibly out of my depth.

'I'm ready to go, Jack,' I repeated, but he didn't hear me. He was staring ahead into the shadows, his eyes locked with a stranger's. 'Jack,' I said a final time, but it was too late; he'd already let go of my hand and disappeared into the darkness.

I woke up alone the next day. I'd walked home from the club by myself, and it had given me time to think. I was a little annoyed that Jack had left me alone in the darkroom, but I'd still enjoyed the experience and was grateful to have tried something new. There was something, however, that didn't feel quite right, and that was the slowly dawning realisation that everything we did here seemed to revolve around Jack.

Jack seemed so certain of who he was, as if he'd already decided on the person he wanted to be, but I hadn't worked that out for myself yet. He had always taught me not to play by somebody else's rulebook, but the sweet irony was that I'd been playing by his rules since I arrived here. Berlin was fun, sure, and I didn't regret being there, but Jack had planned every single moment of every single day. He was the one who'd sent me to Frankfurt and the one who brought me here to Berlin, and while I didn't mind falling through the days, waiting for the next adventure, it was becoming clear that this wasn't *my* adventure – it was *his*.

It was mid-afternoon by the time Jack finally returned to the apartment. He was whistling a happy little tune as he climbed the stairs and swinging a bag of pastries when he came in. He always bought us pastries when he was in a good mood, and I had a sinking feeling of guilt in the bottom of my stomach, knowing I was about to shatter it.

'Good night, then?' I asked as he jumped down on the inflatable mattress, expelling the remaining air inside and flattening it instantly.

'Not even.' He laughed. 'I went home with this muscle twink but he passed out cold before we could even do anything.' He tore open the paper bag, pulled out a pastry and tossed it to me. 'Good kisser though. Got his number, probably won't call him.'

I gave him a weak smile, barely listening to what he was saying. He cocked his head to one side, guessing that I had something to say.

'Did you use protection?' I asked, avoiding the conversation I really wanted to have.

'With which guy?' he said with a grin as he munched on one of the pastries. I was clearly unamused. ''Course I did.' He rolled his eyes. 'Come on, what's really bothering you?'

'I just—' I looked down at the untouched pastry, and then up at Jack again. 'I think it's probably time I head out, go somewhere different.'

'Really?' he said, surprised. 'Why? It's not something I did, is it?'

'No,' I said. It was the truth. 'I just don't really know what I'm doing here.'

Jack looked at me, setting down the pastry and clenching his jaw. It was something he always did when he was thinking.

'But we're having fun, right? I thought we were having fun?'

'We are, Jack. That's exactly it. All we ever do is have fun.'

'Well, that's what life's about, isn't it?' He shrugged his shoulders.

'Not for me. I want something more than that.'

Jack picked up the pastry and began eating it again. I stared at him, waiting for answers or a solution that I knew he wouldn't be able to give.

'Maybe I could come with you?' he said, after a long pause. 'We could go exploring together. Figure it out. Find something new.'

'I think I need to figure this out for myself,' I said, trying to ignore all the happy memories that were rapidly flooding back.

'Well, where are you gonna go?'

'I don't know. Somewhere. Anywhere.'

Jack paused for a moment, staring down at his feet, his jaw clenching and unclenching as he processed everything I'd said, and then he finally gave me a slow reluctant nod. All this time, I'd admired his carefree attitude and his lack of worry, but as he stood in front of me now, it was clear he was as lost as I was.

'I'm gonna miss you,' he finally said.

'I know,' I said. 'I'm gonna miss you too.'

IBIZA

Chapter Eight

I'd taken a lot of flights in my time, but I'd never experienced anything quite like the Friday-night flight from Barcelona to Ibiza. I'd expected the usual strap-in-and-shut-up approach to flying, but this was quite the opposite. It was no more than a thirty-minute flight and everyone was up and out of their seats from the moment the seatbelt light was switched off. The air steward's minibar was drunk dry within minutes, somebody played trance music loudly over a portable speaker and a club promoter even got out of their seat and started wandering down the aisle, handing out leaflets and promising free shots. The spectacle was entertaining, but I remained firmly in my seat, watching the twinkling lights of the city below as we began our approach to the island.

After Berlin, I didn't really know what to do with myself. I still had plenty of money left over from my summer of teaching, and I wanted at least one more adventure before I started looking for another job. Ibiza had always appealed to me – countless friends had been to the island and all come back with stories of misadventure. It seemed like as good a place as any and, keen to live some stories of my own, I booked a flight on a whim and headed towards the infamous party island of legend.

'First time?' the stranger next to me said in a thick Irish accent, spilling his plastic cup of whisky all over himself as he hopped back into his seat.

'Oh, yeah.' I was still staring out of the window, barely realising he was talking to me.

'Business or pleasure?' he continued, trying to dab away the whisky from his otherwise clean white shirt.

'Pleasure, I guess, you?'

'Business. I've lost count of how many times I've been over. I work on a cruise ship, and it's picking me up there tomorrow.' He smiled. 'I'm Colin.'

'Calum,' I said back. I couldn't tell if he was flirting, and although he was incredibly attractive – wavy strawberry-blond hair, a short, trimmed beard and dazzling green eyes – he wasn't really my type. I liked that he spoke enthusiastically about his work, however, and he took the time to ask about me, too. By the time the plane began its descent we were laughing loudly as we swapped stories about our travels.

'Well, let me know if you need a tour guide,' he said as we came to a gradual stop on the runway. He got out of his seat and offered me a handshake.

'Will do.' I smiled and shook his hand, knowing I probably wasn't going to take him up on his offer. I wanted to be his friend, but I was careful not to lead him on.

I didn't think I'd see him again after that. Ibiza may be a small island, but it is still home to over 130,000 people – plenty to get lost among. But fate has a twisted sense of humour – and so of course Colin would be stood outside smoking a cigarette at the exact moment my taxi pulled up at the hotel I'd be staying in.

'Well, hello stranger.' Colin grinned as I slipped out of the cab. 'You're not staying here, are you?' He gestured back to the old and decrepit hotel. 'You've picked the worst hotel on the island.'

'Why are you staying here then?' I laughed.

'Cheap.' He shrugged. 'You coming in?' He dropped his cigarette to the ground and stamped it out before offering to help with my suitcase.

'What room are you in?' he asked as we picked up our keys from the front desk.

'401.' I held up my keys.

'406.' He smiled, raising his key and jangling it. 'We're on the same floor.'

We went up in the lift together. Our rooms were at opposite ends of the same corridor – fate seemed determined to throw us together.

'See you later, then?' Colin said as we parted ways. He went in for a hug just as I went for a handshake, and we fumbled over one another awkwardly.

'Yeah, see you later – nice to see you again.' I walked down the hallway and unlocked the door to my room.

It was basic and ever so slightly dishevelled, but I didn't mind too much. I thought about going over to Colin's room and taking him up on his offer to show me around, but after a long summer of living with other people it felt nice to have my own space. The door to the balcony was broken and wouldn't close properly, but it opened up to clear views out over the harbour and the hustle and bustle of the town below. I sat on the balcony for a few minutes and breathed in the air. I could see drunken tourists everywhere below, but I enjoyed the stillness and quiet of looking down over them from up here, in my little sanctuary.

There was a knock at my door. It had barely been ten minutes and I thought it was a little keen for Colin to come knocking already, but it wasn't him. It was room service, here to drop off an ice bucket and a bottle of prosecco. *Compliments of Room 406.*

I thought about it for a moment and then decided to go down the hall to thank him. I took the prosecco with me. It was the very least I could do.

'Hey.' I smiled, holding up the prosecco and two glasses as he opened the door. 'I was planning to get an early night, but one drink couldn't hurt.'

'An early night?' He laughed and gestured for me to come inside. 'You can't go to bed at 10 p.m. on a Friday night in Ibiza.'

'Just one drink.' I set down the glasses and popped the cork on the bottle. The prosecco bubbled over and stickied up my hands. I poured Colin a glass and followed him out onto his balcony, where we stood together, slightly awkwardly at first, and watched a party boat full of drunk people getting ready to pull out into the Mediterranean. Some of the girls looked like they could barely keep themselves upright, and one of the boys had already fallen over backwards while trying to climb on board.

'I don't really understand the appeal of it,' Colin finally said, gesturing to the row of neon-lit bars that lined the harbour. 'I don't understand why anyone would waste their time on this strip when there's a beautiful island they could be exploring.'

'Well where would you recommend?'

'Depends. What are you in the mood for?'

I don't know if it was his hatred for tourists or his cocky personality, but there was something in him that reminded me of Jack. I started to tell him a bit more about myself: about Matteo, about Jack, and all the travels that had led me here. Colin seemed genuinely interested in what I had to say – leaning in, making heavy eye contact and looking almost as if he wanted to kiss me.

He definitely wanted to kiss me.

'I feel like maybe I need a break from guys, you know?' I said, hoping that I'd dropped an obvious enough hint that I just wanted to be friends.

'Mmhm,' he replied, with absolutely no conviction.

'Honestly, I'm not looking to get with anyone on the island.'

'You never know.' He smiled and started topping up my drink. I didn't know how to tell him I wasn't interested, and to make that clear without seeming rude. But I didn't want to leave him either; I was enjoying his company.

'I've not had the best experience with guys myself,' he added after some time. He told me about a guy he'd met out here just over a year ago, and how they'd fallen in love almost instantly; but with both of them travelling so much, it was never going to work. 'He ended up cheating on me,' he said as we finished the last of the prosecco. 'It wasn't his fault, I guess. We weren't there for each other, I wasn't around and so he went looking for it elsewhere. We broke up a few weeks ago.'

I felt bad for him. His story wasn't so dissimilar from my own – he was lonely, and that was the crux of it. It was something I could relate to. I could hardly blame him for latching on to the first gay guy he saw.

It didn't take long for me to take Colin up on his offer to give me a tour, and so we headed out into the Old Town of Ibiza. I could feel the alcohol kicking in as we walked together in the cool evening air; it was almost midnight, and people were already spilling out of the bars, brawling in the street or throwing up into the harbour. Colin steered me well clear of all of them, leading me uphill and into the quiet of the sleeping town that looked down over the bars below. He pointed out historical landmarks along the way, telling me semi-interesting facts, and even offered his jacket when he noticed that I was shivering in the chill of the evening air.

He finally led me down a winding cobbled street and took me to a rustic-looking bar with a single candle flickering on the window ledge. He told me that this bar belonged to the locals. It was empty apart from a group of four men playing cards in one corner.

'Take a seat,' he said, pointing over to a table by the far window. As I did, I realised why he'd brought me here – the little window opened out to a stunning view of the town below. The distant lights that had seemed so garish up close now glinted like a river of silver and gold. Colin rattled off something in Spanish to the bartender, who handed him a glass bottle from the shelf. '*Gracias,*' he said with terrible pronunciation and then brought the bottle and a pair of ice-filled glasses over to me.

'*Pacharán*,' he said, shaking the bottle. It was unlabelled and filled with a dark purple liquid. 'The pig farmers drink it for courage.' He poured a little over the ice in one of the glasses and handed it to me. 'You know, before they have to gut the pigs.'

'Charming,' I said, breathing in the murky sweetness of the drink as I took a slow and tentative sip. It tasted like warm berries and deodorant.

'Nice, right?' He took a sip himself. 'This stuff's deadly.'

It was probably the alcohol, but Colin had really grown on me by the time we left the bar. He was the perfect gentleman as he guided my woozy self back through the cobbled streets to the hotel. We had to stop by the harbour as I joined the people I'd judged so harshly earlier in throwing up into the clear blue of the Mediterranean.

We were still giddy and giggly when we got back to the hotel, me waving to the receptionist as I tripped over my own feet. The lift brought us back to the fourth floor, where Colin walked me to my door. He let me inside and then gently laid me down on the bed, helping me out of my clothes and kissing me on the forehead as he did. It was a little much, but I didn't mind. I'd be lying if I said I wasn't just a little bit flattered by his advances.

'Goodnight, Colin.' I grinned as I closed my drunken eyes.

That was his cue to leave, but he didn't. I heard the sound of the door click shut, and then the sound of him kicking off his shoes as he climbed in bed beside me.

'I just want to sleep,' I said in a drunken haze, my head throbbing and the room beginning to spin in slow, nauseating circles. 'You need to go back to your own room.'

He tried to put his arms around me then. 'Can I just stay for a little bit?'

'I just want to be alone,' I said.

'Just for a little while?' His voice was now soft and desperate.

'. . . okay.' I was too tired to argue.

I couldn't have been asleep long when I woke up to him kissing me. I tried to pull away, but he pulled me in closer, his coarse stubble grating on my skin.

'Stop.' I pushed him away, a little more aggressively than before, but he was already pulling at my underwear, unbuckling his belt and climbing on top of me. I tried to ask him to stop again, but he didn't, and he started trying to push himself inside of me. I resisted, and he started grinding himself against me until I felt a sickening warmth spatter against my skin.

He lay down beside me, panting and out of breath, his sweaty skin pressing up against mine. He kissed me on the cheek in a way that made me feel sick.

'Please go,' I said, gentler now, my voice beginning to crack a little. Without saying a word, he got back up and left.

Chapter Nine

Colin's shoes were still lying discarded by the bed when I woke up the next morning, a reminder that he'd been there. Dirty brown Chelsea boots. I remember them vividly even now. I thought about returning them by leaving them outside his room, but I threw them in the trash instead.

I was okay – or at least I thought I was. Sometimes I feel like I should've been more upset than I was, but I don't really remember feeling that way. I think it's important to recognise that not everybody reacts to something like this in the same way – some people may internalise the trauma and begin to show signs of depression, whereas others may respond with outbursts of anger, or just feel numb. For me, I just remember feeling sick.

Last night was great he texted me later that morning. *Wanna see me off later?* He finished it with a kiss and a winking face that made me want to scream. Either he was trying to gaslight me, or he genuinely didn't think he'd done anything wrong. I didn't know which was worse, but it was somewhat telling that he never texted me again after that – and he never came looking for his shoes.

I should've reported what happened that night, but I never did. I'd willingly let him take off my clothes and I'd allowed him to sleep in my bed, and that made me feel all the more guilty. I was afraid to tell anyone, and even felt like I was to blame.

This is common – a staggeringly high number of LGBT+ people have experienced some form of sexual violence, and the majority of cases go unreported. From personal anecdotal evidence alone, I can list dozens of examples of stories from friends that are not so different from my own – many of them considerably worse.

We are often so desensitised to being touched and groped inappropriately that we come to expect it and treat it as the norm – I couldn't tell you the last time I went to my local gay club without somebody grabbing me without consent, and that's something that's been consistent throughout my entire adult life. The first time I ever stepped into a gay bar – at just eighteen – a drag queen pulled me in front of a crowd and tried to force her hands into my underwear. It was all supposedly part of the show, and seemed so normalised that everyone just laughed along at the spectacle. My intimidated teenage self laughed along with them – because what else could I do?

I believe that part of the problem is rooted in the lack of education around sex and relationships. If you tell kids that being gay is immoral, how are they supposed to develop healthy sexual boundaries, and understand what constitutes right and wrong? Our society often fails our kids, especially when they're LGBT+, and those kids are growing up into adults whose entire understanding of sex and relationships is flawed. If we don't equip our kids with the right knowledge, how can we expect them to be better?

I thought about what happened that night over and over again, and I didn't want to leave my hotel room until I knew that he was gone. On his cruise ship, off this island and as far away from me as possible. I'd completely lost track of the reason I'd come here in the first place, and instead of spending my time and energy on myself, I was instead focusing all of it on him. I showered three times, trying to scrub all traces of him from my skin, and as soon as the sun went down I ventured outside to buy myself a bottle of wine to try to drown my memory of him in. I think it was anger that I felt then; I'd thought about picking up my phone and berating him on more than one occasion, but the thought of even speaking to him made my skin crawl. I deleted his number and blocked him from contacting me ever again.

I didn't know what else to do or who to reach out to, and so eventually I put on my most revealing outfit, wearing my sexuality like armour, and headed out into town. I knew there was a little pocket of gay bars nearby, and like I had so many times before, I went in search of the comforting arms of my community. Flawed and imperfect as always, but a place that felt like home.

I was a little tipsy from all the wine when I finally spotted the familiar striped rainbow flag bustling in the breeze. It marked a single gay bar tucked away into the quieter part of town. It wasn't very far from the bar we'd visited the night before, but I tried to force myself to live in the present, and to push last night from my mind. There were a few people chatting noisily outside, and I was surprised to hear that they were all speaking in Italian. My head turned whenever I heard that sweet accent, and I couldn't help but try to eavesdrop on their conversation.

'*Bocchino*,' was the only word I heard. *Little mouth*: a euphemism for a blowjob.

One of the boys was really cute: the perfect distraction. I wanted to join their conversation but I knew my Italian was rusty and that I'd never be able to keep up. I lingered for a moment, looking for an opportunity to introduce myself, and then a tall drag queen in a bright green dress came out, looked around and smiled in my direction before ducking back inside.

The drag queens were what I always loved about gay bars. A lot of people find them intimidating, but I've always seen them as the hostesses of our community – always happy to welcome new people, and always happy to make new friends. A friend had told me about a drag queen they'd met out here, Coco, and I wondered if it was her.

I followed her inside and tried to get her attention, but she appeared to be looking for someone and I couldn't catch her eye.

'Coco?' I finally called as she passed me a second time.

'Who, me?' she said in a Spanish accent, looking at me for a moment, puzzled. Her lips turned upwards into a smile. 'You've got the wrong drag queen, honey.'

'Do you know where I can find her?' I asked, not even knowing what I'd say to her if I did. I was just trying to make conversation.

'I don't know anyone by that name,' she said, 'and I know every queen on this island.' She laughed. 'I'm trying to find someone myself. About six foot five, caramel skin and brown eyes you can get lost in. Have you seen him?'

'I don't think so. What's his name?' I asked.

'Any name'll do,' she said, and then laughed at her own terrible joke.

'Oh, don't encourage her,' a man interrupted, rolling his eyes. 'She makes that same damn joke every single week.'

The drag queen pursed her lips and stretched out her gloved hand. 'I'm Carmen, honey. And this old rat is Ricky Riccardo.'

'It's Riccardo,' the man corrected, feigning annoyance.

'Are you new around here?' Carmen asked. She appeared to have given up on finding whoever it was she'd been searching for, and had now turned her attention to me.

'Second night.' I tried not to think about the first.

'Second night and you've already found Carmen!' She smiled. 'You should count your blessings. Come, let me introduce you to a few of my friends.'

She took me by the hand and whisked me outside, back to the Italian boys I'd been eyeing on my way in.

'Boys, boys, boys! Stop talking about your little dicks and come and say hello to my new friend . . .' She paused for a moment. 'What's your name again?'

'Calum,' I said, a little nervously.

'. . . come and say hello to my new friend Calum,' she continued. 'He's better-looking than all of you put together, and I can already tell that he's packing.'

Carmen might as well have picked me up and thrown me at the Italian boys, because before I knew it she'd disappeared back into the bar and they'd surrounded me.

'She's a real character, right?' one of the boys said.

'She sure is something,' I replied. 'What are your names?'

'Valerio.' 'Davide.' 'Simone.' 'Matteo.'

Matteo. Of course the prettiest of the bunch was called Matteo. I guess it's a common name, but it struck me all the same. He was older than the one I'd known in Italy – by perhaps five or six years – but his bouncy black hair and the way he grinned seemed intangibly familiar. If I didn't know better, I'd have guessed he was his brother.

'I knew a boy called Matteo once,' I said. It had been months since I last saw him, but I still thought about him almost every day. I wondered what he was doing then, and imagined him, Gianmarco and Gabriele doing something stupendously idiotic.

'I miss him,' I added, realising there hadn't been any point in bringing him up.

'Were you in love?' one of the boys asked.

'He was too young. But I cared about him very much.'

'Maybe one day?' Ibiza Matteo asked. I shook my head.

'I think that ship has sailed.'

'Well, where are you going later then?' he said. 'Do you want to come out with us? We're going to Space – it's full of tourists, but we do love an English boy.'

'Is it a gay club?' I asked.

'*Is it a gay club*?!' they repeated in unison, laughing but not answering the question.

'Everyone's a little bit gay in Ibiza,' one of them finally said.

We knocked back a few more drinks at the bar before heading out. As we left, another guy chased after us, pulling on his jacket as he caught up.

'Hey, how you doing?' I smiled, confidently greeting the newcomer. 'I'm Calum.'

He looked at me blankly. 'Honey, it's Carmen – we met a whole twenty minutes ago. How many drinks did you give her?' he answered, playfully hitting me as he did. Carmen looked so different out of drag – he was beautiful as a woman and even more beautiful as a man.

We piled into a cab that spiralled us out of the little town, taking us down the east coast and to what remains the biggest nightclub I've ever been to. An impossibly long queue of people snaked outside the front, but Carmen took my hand and led me straight to the front door. The doorman let us through without so much as blinking.

'We don't queue with the tourists,' Carmen said with a wink as he took me inside.

The interior of the club was like a city of its own. The ceiling was so high that you'd forget you were indoors, and there were so many different bars that the whole place felt like its own little metropolis.

'It's a lot to take in, huh?' Carmen said as I looked around, wide-eyed. A seizure of a light show exploded above us as a DJ wearing a giant foam mask bounced up and down in front of a hyped and heaving crowd.

Carmen led me and the Italian boys through the club and to another oversized dance floor.

'Feeling drunk enough?' he asked. 'Because the drinks here will cost you more than your health. A single vodka costs twenty euros.'

'I think I could do with a drink, actually,' I said, looking over towards the bar. I smiled as I caught the eye of a guy waiting to be served, who had streaky blond surfer hair and wore a sleeve-less tank top that showed off his body.

'She's been here two minutes and she's already pulled!' Carmen mockingly rolled his eyes. 'We'll leave you to it, honey. Come find us when you're done,' he said, and without a second look they'd already vanished into the crowd.

The surfer guy had overheard them and was now laughing to himself. He mimed the universally accepted hand gesture for a drink, to which I nodded and mouthed 'please'.

'What can I get you?' he said in a South African accent as I squeezed in beside him.

'Are you sure? I hear a vodka will set you back twenty euros.'

'Everything in Ibiza will set you back twenty euros.' He laughed.

'Well, thanks,' I said as the bartender handed him a beer. 'I'll have the same.' The bartender flipped open another beer and handed it to me.

'Forty,' he said, gesturing the number four with his fingers.

'It's a playground for the rich and stupid,' the South African said after he'd handed over the money, and waved his arm towards the crowd of heaving ravers. 'Nobody here is drinking, that's the problem. The alcohol's more expensive than the drugs.'

'Well, when in Ibiza . . .'

'Have you got any?'

I shook my head. I'd never taken any party drugs before; the most I'd ever taken was a space cake in Amsterdam. 'Maybe later tonight,' I added, taking myself by surprise.

I hadn't even considered it until that moment, but something about being there made me want to try it.

'Good for you!' the South African said, clinking his beer against mine. 'Fancy a dance?' he offered, nodding over to the surging crowd.

'I thought you said they were all rich idiots?'

'They are. I'm a rich idiot too.' He winked.

'Maybe later then.' I laughed, but he was already pulling away.

'Later,' he agreed, raising his beer in the air as he let the crowd consume him.

Chapter Ten

Everyone in the club seemed to have come to the island for the exact same reason – to forget about reality, to drink, fuck, take drugs and have fun. That's why I was so open to the idea when a stranger tapped me on the shoulder and offered to sell me drugs. I wanted to push myself beyond my comfort zone; I wanted to try something entirely different.

'Ecstasy?' I said, not really knowing what I was asking for.

'Forty,' he replied without a smile. I took out a pair of twenties and slipped them to him. He double-checked the money and then passed me a tiny rolled-up piece of cling film, and without even looking at it, I slipped it into my pocket.

'Thanks,' I said, but he'd already turned and gone in the other direction.

I wandered through the crowds for a few minutes, taking in the music and constantly reaching into my pocket to check that the little packet was still there. I eventually pushed through into one of the countless bathrooms and waited for a cubicle. I'm pretty sure that's what everyone was doing in there anyway;

people were wiping their noses so blatantly as they came out in twos and threes that they might as well have just done it right there on the sinks.

I didn't have to wait too long and finally got inside one of the cubicles, pushing the door closed behind me. The top of the toilet had remnants of white powder on it and half a black straw that had been politely left for the next person. I emptied my pockets and looked down at the small brown pill wrapped inside the cling film. I had no idea how to take it – do I crush it, snort it, eat it or put it in my drink? I thought of all the movies I'd seen of happy-go-ravers letting pills dissolve on their tongues, and wondered if that was what I was supposed to do.

I needed to find Carmen.

I wrapped the pill back up, pushed it back into my pocket and left the cubicle awkwardly, flushing the toilet and pretending to buckle up my belt, feeling like everyone was watching me. It took a while to find Carmen, but I found him standing alone on a huge smoking terrace upstairs. He looked eternally fabulous as he blew rings of smoke into the night.

'How was your surfer friend?' he asked as he saw me approaching.

'Oh, he was fine.' I smiled back. I'd completely forgotten about the guy I'd met earlier.

'Good kisser?' he asked. I shrugged. 'A time-waster then?'

'He bought me a drink.'

'And so he should have.' Carmen grinned. 'And what have you got there?'

He gestured to the hand I had firmly stuffed into my pocket.

'I got some stuff,' I said, trying perhaps a little too hard to sound like someone who knew the lingo. Carmen raised his eyebrow as I took the cling film out of my pocket and showed it to him as discreetly as I could.

'Where did you get this?' he asked.

'I bought it,' I said, oddly proud of myself.

'From who? From a stranger? Did you try it?'

'No,' I said nervously. 'Was I supposed to?'

'Have you ever taken drugs before, sweetie?' His voice didn't seem at all condescending, but full of genuine concern.

'No,' I said, 'but I thought maybe you guys might want to—'

'Oh honey, we *do*, but we brought some with us, and there's enough for you as well.' He took the cling film out of my hand and flicked it off the balcony. 'Don't ever take candy from strangers.' His voice was now decidedly more pointed.

'But *you're* a stranger,' I protested.

'I'm not a stranger. I'm your good friend Carmen, and I wouldn't let a damned thing happen to even one of those pretty little hairs on your beautiful little head.' He squeezed my bicep affectionately and tapped me on the head. 'Come on.'

We didn't go back into the bathroom, but he pulled me to a quiet corner of the terrace and took out a small white tab from his wallet. He bit down into it, splitting it into four, and placed a piece in my palm.

'Are you sure it's safe?' I asked, looking down at the pill in my hand.

'It's drugs, honey. It's never safe, but it's sure as hell safer than that other crap you were gonna take.'

'What will happen? What will it feel like?'

'It'll feel good, but just take a quarter and see how you feel. You can have a little more later on.' Carmen took his quarter pill in his teeth with a smile and then swallowed it back as I followed suit.

'Shall we go dance?' he asked, stretching out his hand. I took it. I liked how he made me feel attractive and wanted, but not in a way that seemed like he was making a move on me. I felt like he genuinely just wanted to have a good time.

The dance floor was so big that when you looked up you felt like you were staring into the night sky. Confetti cannons went off in every direction as giant beach balls and colossal inflatable animals bounced their way through the crowd.

The music was so intense I could feel it pulsing through me as Carmen pulled me through the crowds. There were a lot of straight couples but I spotted a couple of guys making out with each other, too. It was comforting to see and it let me know that I was free to be myself here as well. Carmen kept yelling things into my ear but I couldn't make out a word, and just laughed and nodded and bounced along with the music.

I thought the drugs weren't working at first. It took a long time for anything to happen, but when it did, everything seemed to happen at once: I felt a warmth rushing through my body, then an overwhelming sense of happiness; my jaw clenched as the music throbbed and then everything suddenly seemed more bright, more colourful, and I felt as though all my troubles had ceased to exist. I put my hands up into the air and waved them around, and I could feel the lasers dancing between my fingers as I tried to catch them. I must have been grinning like a Cheshire cat, and when I looked over to Carmen I saw that he was grinning too.

'Are you coming up?' he yelled into my ear. I nodded, at which he grabbed my face with both hands, pulled it into his and kissed me hard on the mouth – a kiss of friendship, of feeling alive, of sharing this moment together.

I clung on to him and felt my fingers running along his body, wanting to touch every inch of him. The sensations felt incredible as I ran my fingers along his chest and kissed him on the cheek again and again. Another pair of guys bounced over to us, and without saying anything we started dancing and touching and hugging one another. The whole crowd seemed to be in a happy drug-addled stupor.

'I love you,' I shouted to Carmen through the music.

'Honey, you just met me.' He grinned back. 'But I love you all the same.'

He kissed me again, longer this time, and then he turned and kissed one of the boys who were dancing with us. The other one leaned in and kissed me too. I was pretty sure they weren't even gay – just happy, perhaps, and very, very high.

We must have been dancing for hours, but it all went by in a flash. I remember the Italian boys joining us for a bit too. I'm pretty sure that I kissed Ibiza Matteo at some point – and that I was thinking about the other Matteo as I did.

The sun was starting to come up when we finally made our way out of the club. I bounced up and down on the pavement, feeling intensely alert and in control, but in reality I probably had very little control at all.

'I'm alive, awake, alert, enthusiastic,' I cheerily sang. It was one of the songs I'd sing with my students. I remember forcing Ginevra and Giovanni and the others to sing this first thing in the morning, and they absolutely hated me for it.

'I think it's time to put you down for the night,' Carmen said, laughing, as I linked his arm and the arm of a guy we'd probably only just met.

'How about we watch the sunrise first?' I interjected, waving at the deep red that was starting to fill up the early-morning sky. 'Aren't we near the beach?'

'Well, since it's your first time . . .' Carmen smiled and turned us round in the opposite direction. 'It's not very far from here.'

I could feel myself starting to come back down to earth as we made our way to the beach. Palm trees lined the seafront and a mild chill crept in from the waves gently lapping the shore. We kicked off our shoes and held them in our hands as we playfully ran along the white sand, wetting our feet in the water and collapsing in a bundled heap of queer friendship. We lay there for what seemed like a lifetime, listening to the peaceful silence that surrounded us, occasionally talking to check that the others were still awake. Eventually, finally, we drifted off to sleep.

The beach was still deserted when we woke up. We couldn't have been asleep for long, but fortunately I was completely hangover-free. Carmen asked if I wanted to take a walk and I obliged, saying goodbye to the others as we strolled off along the sand.

The drugs must have still been in my system, but I felt considerably mellower – relaxed, but still feeling an overwhelming affection for Carmen. It wasn't entirely the drugs, of course – he really was lovely and I wanted to be his friend. The drugs simply amplified the trust and adoration I was feeling for him.

'You're having a good time on the island?' he asked, breaking the silence as we walked, taking my hand in his.

'Yeah.' I smiled. 'Tonight, at least,' I added, almost stopping myself.

'Oh, yeah?' he said softly, giving me that same look of concern he'd given me earlier.

'I-I met a guy on the first night. And he was a little bit . . . forceful.'

I said it with a meek smile, the kind you give when you're trying to pretend everything's okay. Carmen mulled over this for a minute, his lips twitching. I could tell that he was saddened, but not shocked. He'd have heard different versions of this same story a thousand times before.

'Do you want to talk about it?' he asked. I shook my head. I'd already said all that I needed to. I didn't want to share the details, and I didn't see how it would help.

'It's happened to me before. A few times actually,' Carmen continued. 'Especially when I'm in drag, they get a little handsy, and think they have the right to touch you.'

'I'm sorry.' I didn't know what else to say.

'You never have to do anything you don't want to, Calum,' he said, squeezing my hand a little tighter now. He wasn't looking at me directly, but straight ahead onto the horizon. 'I've learned that the hard way.'

His jaw clenched as he said it, and I knew there was something buried underneath those words – a secret that I knew was painful, without him even needing to share it. Neither of us went into detail that morning about what had happened to us, but it still made me feel infinitely better to have said something.

I wish stories like these were unusual, but countless friends have told me so many that are exactly the same. That they've woken up drunk with someone on top of them, or someone who wouldn't take no for an answer. They'd tell me about first dates where they felt pressured into it, and other times where they wanted to stop halfway through but felt they had to carry on. The worst thing about it is that so many of them blame themselves for what happened – exactly like I did.

'You're allowed to not be okay about this,' Carmen said after a long and painful silence. 'You're allowed to be upset, and you're allowed to be angry.'

But the truth is that I didn't feel either of those things. I felt almost guilty that I didn't, but mostly I just felt numb. We walked along the beach for maybe another twenty minutes without saying anything else, but just having somebody with me who understood me lifted the weight from my shoulders, and made me feel a little better.

'You're a really lovely person, Carmen,' I finally said, breaking the silence that had caught up with us.

'I am, aren't I?' Carmen grinned and let go of my hand. 'Fancy a swim?'

He nodded to the boardwalk ahead, as if trying to distract me, and started to take his clothes off.

'Not right now.' I laughed softly. He stopped and veered us back towards town, where he helped me into a taxi and even paid the driver up front. He jumped into the backseat with me, and as the taxi drove us back up the coast to the Old Town, I lay down in his lap and held his hand.

'You gonna be okay getting back to your room?' he asked when we arrived outside the hotel.

'Yeah,' I said, and smiled as he kissed me on the cheek.

'Take care of yourself, Calum,' he added, as if we were saying goodbye for good.

'I will.' I watched him leave, before sleepily climbing back to my room to fall into a thoughtful sleep.

I decided to take a break from nightlife after that; going out on the LGBT+ club scene definitely seemed like the easiest way to meet people, but I knew it was time to take a step back and focus on other things instead. I went back to Germany and took up another teaching job and found fulfilment in once again working with young and inspiring minds. I even contacted Jack and asked him if he wanted to visit, but he was already halfway round the world by then – already caught up in his next big adventure.

When I finished working in Germany, I took the money that I'd earned and spent a few months travelling through Amsterdam, Budapest, Paris, Prague and Vienna. I slept on trains and in hostels and stayed with old friends and people I'd just met. It was a strange feeling to always be moving forwards, never knowing where I was going next, but it was wonderfully freeing to be able to go anywhere and do anything that I pleased.

I understood that this was a privilege few got to enjoy, and so I seized the opportunity with both hands by applying for jobs all over the world. I applied for anything and everything, from jobs working as a ski instructor to jobs dressing up as an elf in Santa's grotto. I was offered both of those jobs – but I turned them down, because something even more exciting came up instead.

When asked what my dream job was when I was just five years old, I proudly told my parents that I wanted to be a zookeeper. I never thought in a million years that such a dream would ever come true. The job was helping to take care of the animals in a tiger sanctuary, and they wanted me to fly straight out to Thailand to start in a couple of weeks.

The fastest way to get there from central Europe was to have a stopover in India – and so I figured, why kill a few weeks here when I could spend some time in India instead?

INDIA

Chapter Eleven

Homosexuality had just been decriminalised in India. I knew that because I'd looked it up. It was something I always did when visiting a new country – something you have to do when you're LGBT+ – because it's still illegal to be gay in seventy-three countries around the world, and some of those countries still carry the death penalty. Tom and I had naïvely visited Morocco when we were teenagers, and neither of us had realised that our very existence was illegal there until we were already in the country. We could've been given three years in prison just for kissing or holding hands, and that absolutely terrified me. I've checked the status of every single country I've visited ever since.

I don't know what I expected when I arrived in New Delhi, but I was hoping to experience something different. I was definitely a little naïve to what India was really like, though, and I had no idea how hard the culture shock was about to hit me. As I stepped out of the air-conditioned terminal the stagnant heat of the night surrounded me. Everything was so much louder here – drivers blaring their horns and people talking loudly and quickly and seemingly all at once. The taxi rank was a wall of noise as people tried to persuade me into their unofficial-looking taxis; I ignored them and looked for a licensed radio taxi instead. They seemed to be far and few between, and with no sign of any real queuing system, I beelined for the first one I saw, throwing my suitcase into the boot and then hopping into the backseat.

'Where are you headed, sir?' the driver said with a smile, adjusting his music down slightly as he turned round in his seat to face me. I pulled out the address of my hotel and read it to him, and he tilted his head to each side with agreement.

'How much?' I asked, noticing that the meter wasn't running, and in fact didn't seem to be working at all. That should have been my first clue that something was up, but the man seemed to be smiling so innocently that I went along with it anyway.

'Seven thousand,' he answered quickly. I'd looked up the price in advance and knew I shouldn't be paying any more than five hundred rupees for the short trip, and so I began aggressively haggling the price. We finally agreed on seven hundred, but the taxi didn't start moving; he stayed firmly parked, tapping his hands on the steering wheel as if waiting for something to happen.

'Everything okay?' I asked. He assured me that everything was fine, but that's when a man pulled open the passenger-side door and climbed inside. Strange, but nothing to worry about, I thought – and then a second man jumped in the back.

'Don't worry.' The driver smiled, making eye contact with me in his rear-view mirror. 'Just a couple of friends heading in the same direction. We'll get you to your destination shortly,' he added, and with that the car started moving.

I instantly knew that something wasn't right. I don't know why I didn't get out there and then, to seek safety in numbers while we were still surrounded by people. I tried to convince myself that maybe everything was okay, that maybe it was normal to share a taxi like this in India. I kept a smile plastered to my face, worried about how they might react if they realised I knew something was wrong.

I tried to calm myself down as we barrelled down the motor-way at full speed: I was probably overthinking this – perhaps they genuinely were his friends, and he really was giving them a lift into the city. It certainly seemed plausible – and yet the silence in the taxi unnerved me. Not one of them had said a word.

The motorway was something pulled straight from a fever dream. I'd heard rumours about the motorways in India: fellow travellers had told me stories about them as I passed from city to city, but I only ever half-believed them to be true. One person told me that they'd witnessed a pile-up first hand after a group of cows had strayed onto the road, and another told me that her brother had come off his moped and that the paramedics had tried to zip him into a body bag while he was still alive. I never believed the motorways could be as dangerous as people had suggested, but if anything, they turned out to be worse. The motorway was a mish-mash of vehicles and animals all scram-bling around at different speeds, swerving in and out of each other with reckless abandon while blaring their horns inces-santly. It was an accident waiting to happen, and I was amazed that one of the speeding trucks didn't plough right into us as we clumsily darted in between them.

I was tired from the flight but I was so far out of my comfort zone that the adrenaline kept me awake. Very aware that I was on the other side of the world to everyone I knew, I was terrified of all the things that could go wrong. How easily I could disappear.

'You pay now,' the driver suddenly said as we continued to barrel down the motorway. He'd taken his eyes completely off the road to watch me in the mirror.

'Oh,' I said, confused. 'Can I just pay you when we get there?'

'You pay now,' he insisted with an unnerving smile. 'Seven thousand.'

'We agreed seven hundred.' My voice had started to quake. He was asking for the equivalent of around £100 for what should have been a 15-minute journey.

'It's seven thousand,' he repeated. 'You pay now, or you get out.'

'I don't even have that much.' It was the truth, but the driver just broke his eye contact with me and stared dead ahead at the road.

'Okay,' he said. He wasn't agreeing with me. The person in the backseat lunged straight across at me – I thought he was trying to grab me at first, but he reached for the handle to the door instead. We were going at full speed down the motorway and he was trying to open my door.

'Wait, stop!' I fumbled, pushing his hand away just as the door swung open beside me. I reached across to pull it shut, my seatbelt the only thing stopping me from toppling out onto the motorway. I managed to get the door closed again, but the man unclicked my seatbelt and went for the door a second time.

'Stop!' I yelled again, panicking as I reached into my pocket to pull out my wallet. 'I don't have seven thousand,' I said, 'but here, take what I've got.' I started pulling notes out of my wallet and tried to hand them to the guy leaning over me, but he didn't take them, and instead looked to the driver, who gave him a quiet little nod of acknowledgement. The car jolted again and we swerved through the speeding traffic to pull over in the pitch-black darkness at the side of the road.

'Out,' the driver said, leaving the engine running and the headlights on full beam. The three of them opened their doors and got out of the car in unison, as if this had been rehearsed – this wasn't the first time they'd done this.

I stayed firmly in my seat, watching the cars zooming past at full speed. I could get out and make a run for it, but where would I go? I could scream and call for help, but who was going to hear me? I wanted to phone the police, but I didn't even know the number. In India, it's 112. I wish I knew that then.

I didn't move from my seat until they pulled my suitcase from the boot of the car and tossed it into a ditch at the side of the road. That suitcase had my every worldly possession inside – my degree certificate, my old photographs, the teddy bear my parents had given me on the day I was born. I wasn't about to let it all be discarded.

They were on me the moment I opened the door and stepped out of the car. The three of them surrounded me, not saying a word, and the driver held out his hand. I took out my wallet, pulled out the rupees I had and handed them to him. Five thousand rupees, ten times the amount I should have paid – but he still wasn't satisfied. He snatched the wallet from my hand and flicked through it, taking the British pounds, euros, dollars and Thai baht I had as well, and then tossed it back at me. They got back in the car and drove off, leaving me there in the middle of nowhere.

They'd left me with my phone – perhaps it was too difficult to sell, or perhaps it was an act of mercy, but either way it didn't work here. I think that was probably the most afraid I've ever been in my entire life: I trembled and I wanted to cry, but somehow I wasn't able to. It was like I'd been stifled by how completely hopeless I felt.

Not knowing what else to do, I climbed down into the ditch, wrestled my suitcase from the mud and began trying to wave down one of the hundreds of cars that were speeding past me. I wasn't even sure if they could see me in the darkness, but I kept trying anyway – what else could I do? I could've been stuck there all night, and probably would've been if it wasn't for the kindness of one elderly stranger.

Half an hour had passed when I spotted him in his little yellow-and-green tuk-tuk. He came rolling down the road at a much slower pace than the cars that sped around him, and he veered towards me almost instantly to pull up at the side of the road, where he jumped out and asked if I was okay. He told me he'd seen this happen hundreds of times over the years – foreigners stripped of their money and left at the side of the road. He'd picked up a young American couple once who had been stranded here, just like me.

To add insult to injury, it turns out they hadn't just taken my money and left me here; they'd driven me in the wrong direction too, away from the heart of New Delhi. A pointless and malicious cruelty that I don't think I'll ever understand.

'You need a ride?' the old man said, a smile now appearing on his lips. I nodded silently, still shaken from what had happened as he helped me lift my suitcase onto the floor of the tiny tuk-tuk. I felt incredibly exposed as he started the engine. The little vehicle spluttered onto the motorway, and to the man's amusement, I clung on for dear life as we began weaving a path through the speeding traffic.

I started to relax a little as soon as we came off the motorway and began to drive into the city. The streets here were quiet and we pretty much had the roads entirely to ourselves. It wasn't what I expected at all – I'd expected skyscrapers and bright lights, but the city here seemed strangely dark and quiet, almost like a ghost town.

A pack of wild dogs crossed our path, our little headlights illuminating their eyes in the darkness and scaring them back into the shadows. There were homeless people too – more homeless people than I'd ever seen in one place – huddling together under bridges and in alleyways, anywhere that served as a shelter. It was this poverty that stood out to me more than anything; the divide between the rich and poor was striking, and I couldn't help feeling that I was somehow contributing to it by having booked a five-star hotel for my stay. It was a tall and – it now seemed to me – unnecessarily grandiose building that loomed over the city, sparkling with twinkling lights, seeming so at odds with everything that surrounded it.

The driver pulled in and gave me a little card with his name and number on it, and told me to give him a call if I ever needed a ride. I reached down into my sock to pull out the few hundred rupees I had stashed there. It was something my grandma had always insisted upon: always keep emergency money in your sock. I'd done it since I was little, but I never thought I'd ever actually need it. It was thanks to her that I was able to offer to pay this kind and generous stranger. He shook his head as I held out the sweaty-sock money, however, and refused to take it, waving me away with a little laugh as he climbed back into his tuk-tuk and revved its little engine.

It was 2 a.m. now and I was ready to get to my room, lock the door and collapse. I felt like I hadn't taken a deep breath since I got here, and I just wanted the comfort and safety of my own private space. Music was playing in the lobby as I walked in, and the scent of warm spices wafted through the air. The smartly dressed lady on the front desk smiled warmly as I approached, and seemed incredibly concerned when I told her what had happened. She asked if I'd got the number plate of the taxi, and I felt stupid when I told her that it hadn't even occurred to me.

'Let's get you checked in anyway.' She smiled and started pulling up my booking reference. I thought everything had been paid in advance, but she said that it hadn't, and asked me for my credit card. I handed it over – thankfully the muggers hadn't taken it – but in keeping with my bad luck that night, the transaction was declined.

'I called the bank to tell them I was coming,' I said as she tried the card again and it was rejected a fourth, and then a fifth time. 'Can I just check in and sort this out tomorrow?'

She shook her head apologetically and handed back my card.
'I can't check you in without payment, I'm afraid. Company policy,' she said. 'There's an ATM down the street – maybe you could try that?'

'I'll give it a try,' I said. I didn't want to go back out onto the streets in the middle of the night, but what else could I do? I left my suitcase behind in the reception and resigned myself to going out to try to find the ATM.

I was so on edge as I made my way back out into the darkness that every little sound made me jittery. My own shadow would've scared me and so it's no surprise that I almost jumped out of my skin when a voice called out from behind.

'Hey!' I spun round to see a young man dressed in a suit running down the hotel steps. 'You're not having the best night, are you?' he chuckled. 'Are you okay?'

He came over and placed a friendly hand onto my shoulder. His name was Vibhor, and he was a junior member of the hotel staff. He had a gentle smile and kind, inquisitive eyes, and had I not been so shaken from everything that was happening, I probably would've stopped to notice how attractive he was.

'I just need to get to the ATM,' I said, and he bobbled his head from side to side. It was an Indian gesture I'd grow to love – it could mean any one of a thousand things, but above all else, it meant that the person was listening, and a sign that they'd understood.

'I'll take you, don't worry,' he answered sympathetically.

My favourite thing about Vibhor was his ability to talk at length about absolutely anything – give him a topic and he could talk for hours. He used this skill to distract me as he guided me down the street. It was a much longer walk than I'd expected, and although Vibhor didn't look particularly tough, I felt a lot safer with him beside me.

We finally reached the ATM at the end of the street, and there, surrounded by looming cast-iron gates, was a blinking neon sign offering free 24-hour cash withdrawals.

'It's not usually closed,' Vibhor said, shaking the padlocked gates with frustration. 'I guess we're going to have to climb.'

I looked at him with disbelief, unsure that I'd heard him correctly.

'Come,' he continued, and hoisted himself up onto the dirty and greasy railings, tarnishing his perfectly pressed suit as he did.

'Are you sure?' I said with a little reluctance as I followed him, but Vibhor was already pulling himself over the top, tearing his suit jacket on the spikes as he did.

The ATM blinked expectantly as I jumped down on the other side, but just as I had suspected, it rejected my request for a withdrawal over and over again.

'I just need to call my bank,' I said. 'But the banks back home won't open for another . . . twelve hours,' I added, puzzling at my watch, trying to calculate the time difference.

'Don't worry,' Vibhor responded cheerily, leading me back towards the hotel. 'You're with Vibhor now, and as long as you're with Vibhor, everything will be okay.'

It turned out that Vibhor and I were exactly the same age – we were both twenty-two and even shared the same birthday – and on discovering this he excitedly claimed that he knew there was a reason he was drawn to me. Having the same birthday, however, was where the similarities ended: he was married, lived locally and had never stepped outside of India. Being a family man was all he ever wanted, and to him, family was everything.

'And do you have a partner?' he asked, careful with his choice of words. I shook my head. I thought about concealing my sexuality from him, but I wanted to keep the promise I'd made to myself when I left Italy, and so I told him the truth. He nodded with a quiet understanding when I said it, turning it over in his mind for a few moments, but I was worried that I was making him uncomfortable and so I quickly changed the subject.

I didn't know what I expected to happen when we walked back into the hotel, but Vibhor must have had more authority than he'd let on. After a quick conversation with the lady on the desk, he came back with a key card and a cup of hot chai.

'We've got a room for you,' he said, handing me the tea and walking me towards the elevators. 'The penthouse was empty so we've put you in there. I've already sent up your bag. It really is the least we could do.'

'Thank you, Vibhor.' I didn't know what strings he'd pulled or why, but I couldn't be more grateful for this incredible act of kindness.

'You're very welcome, sir,' he said. 'Maybe I'll see you tomorrow?'

'I hope so,' I said. 'Goodnight, Vibhor.'

'Goodnight, sir,' he said, and pushed the button for the twenty-first floor.

Chapter Twelve

I woke up in paradise. The room had floor-to-ceiling windows, and without even getting up from the giant four-poster bed, I had panoramic views right out over the city. The sun was just beginning to rise, and it gently warmed my skin as it blazed in through the windows and illuminated the city below. It felt like I had woken up somewhere completely different, the city now full of colour and so much more vibrant than it had seemed in the dead of night. The sun dazzled over India Gate, the grand arch in the centre of the city, and birds danced circles in the warm currents of the early-morning air.

I climbed out of bed and looked down to the ant-sized people bustling through the streets below, setting up their market stalls and bringing the city to life. It was completely unrecognisable, and for the first time since I'd arrived, I was really glad to be there.

I got up and pulled open the balcony door; even all the way up there the sweetness of spices in the air still hit me as I stepped outside and inhaled a sharp and grateful breath. The most beautiful song could be heard faintly in the distance, the call to prayer, and although I've never been a religious person, I felt truly privileged to be in a city that seemed to live and breathe its many religions.

Not wanting to waste any more time, I showered, got dressed and made my way downstairs to find breakfast. I wanted to find Vibhor as well, to thank him again for all his kindness. He wasn't in the lobby, but I found him in the restaurant talking to a couple with a big and friendly smile on his face. He greeted me with enthusiasm when he spotted me, telling me that the room was taken care of for the rest of the week and that I needn't worry about anything. It was then that I found out that his parents owned the hotel, and suddenly everything made sense.

It was one of those many remarkably fortuitous things that happened to me on my travels, and it sometimes made me feel like there was someone, or something, watching over me. I'd been so lucky that the kind tuk-tuk driver had spotted me by the side of the road, and even luckier that Vibhor had been in the hotel lobby when I got there. Things could've wound up very differently otherwise. It was a silver lining if there ever was one – the room would've cost far more than the amount of money I'd had stolen – and I'd even made a new friend as well.

'Get yourself some breakfast,' Vibhor said, pointing at the grand buffet that awaited me. 'My shift finishes at two; maybe I can show you around?'

'I'd love that,' I said, and he clasped his hands together in agreement.

'See you later then,' he said with a grin, and headed towards the lobby to check on some more guests. I still wasn't sure what his job was; I think he just liked to help out.

The buffet that awaited me was the most extravagant I'd ever seen. Rotis were stacked high alongside bowls of sweetened rice and tapioca, and there were piles of fresh fruit and pastries and all kinds of things I'd never before laid eyes on. I had no idea how to eat any of it, and so I cobbled together a small plate of things that probably didn't complement one another.

I sat down by a window with a view of the palatial gardens outside. I people-watched as I sat there, wondering who the other guests were. I made up stories about them in my mind – that family was having a holiday in the city, and that one was probably accompanying their father as he came into town for business. I most enjoyed watching a huge wedding party that had been mingling in the foyer: the men came in first, chatting noisily in their intricately gilded outfits, followed closely by the women in their sparkling jewels and long, flowing saris. The women were in splashes of pink and orange, and the men formed a backdrop of sapphire, ivy and gold. There was a pair of little girls decorated with bindis and lotus flowers, and a young mother quietly fussed over her adorable infant son as he tugged at his now misshapen turban. The room was a carnival of colours – even the businessmen were wearing shirts of lavender and rose beneath their pastel-coloured suits. From the food to the clothing to the wild flowers that grew in every crack and crevice, from the painted vehicles that cluttered the streets to the graffiti that spiralled across the walls, India seemed to have an obsession with colour – and I absolutely loved it.

I really enjoyed sitting there, silently watching – as an introvert at heart, taking some time to centre myself was everything that I needed. Despite my dramatic introduction to India, being here now was exactly what I'd been craving. I took my time with my breakfast, and then headed out with no destination in mind. I just wanted to take a stroll and gently immerse myself in the city.

The streets were now alive with tuk-tuks and rickshaws speeding up and down. Pop-up market stalls were scattered along the sides of the roads, and cattle roamed freely, meandering among the people going about their business. Everyone smiled at me as I walked by, browsing the various market stalls and looking at the unfamiliar food they had on display. I didn't know what any of it was, but I wanted to try everything. I'd been warned about eating the street food here and getting the infamous Delhi Belly that turned foreigners' stomachs to mush, but how could I come all the way here and not?

I decided getting sick was a chance worth taking, and made quick work of trying everything in sight. I was amazed at how cheap it all was – I felt like a rich man as I walked through the streets, and realised that was exactly why I'd been targeted the night before. I'd be lying if I said I wasn't a little apprehensive about that happening again, but the overwhelming sense of kindness I now felt encouraged me to relax into my surroundings.

I spent another hour exploring the city and eventually circled back to the hotel to see if Vibhor had finished his shift, mapping out the city in my mind as I retraced my every step. I was excited to spend the rest of the day with him, and to get his perspective on the city that he called home.

He was sitting on the steps of the hotel when I arrived. He was wearing an oversized white T-shirt, jeans and a baseball cap, and he looked so different out of his suit, somehow even friendlier. He jumped up when he saw me and pulled me into a hug.

'You seem a little happier now,' he said, and I gave him a little nod.

'It's not so bad here after all.'

He chuckled. 'It is my home,' he said modestly, gesturing to the city around us. 'Tell me. Where would you like to go first?'

Vibhor opened up to me pretty quickly as we walked through the city. He told me about his wife Amrit, and about how their marriage had been arranged by their parents. He was Hindu, and he told me about their wedding with enormous enthusiasm. I later learned that his name quite literally means 'enthusiastic' in Hindi, and I couldn't think of a name more fitting. It was definitely enlightening talking to him – I knew that arranged marriages existed, but I didn't realise how common they were. Pretty much everyone he knew had entered an arranged marriage shortly after leaving school, and he said that he and his friends were quite content with the wives their parents had chosen for them.

'It's just the way things are done,' he said. 'It's tradition. Love marriages aren't so common here because love is something you build, not something that you stumble into.' He told me that he'd first seen Amrit in a photograph, and admitted that it was difficult for her at first, as it hadn't been a marriage of love.

'With life you learn to love someone for the good qualities they have,' he said. 'And Amrit and I learn to love one another with every day that passes.'

I wanted to believe that Vibhor was a good husband: he always lit up when he talked about his wife, and he spoke at length about her beauty and her talents and their unconditional friendship. I wish I could have met Amrit, to see that she was happy, to see that she, too, was content with the husband who had been chosen for her.

We continued walking until we reached Lodhi Gardens, a magnificent garden that bloomed in the heart of the city. Exotic trees blossomed and wild colourful birds darted among their branches, the fresh scent of honeydew lingering as happy couples breathed in the air. Rows of symmetrical fountains lined the lily-pad streams that cut between the overgrowth, and crumbling stone bridges gave way to hidden passages through the trees.

'This is my favourite place in all of Delhi,' Vibhor told me. 'I sometimes come here to write.' Like me, he wanted to be an author, and he excitedly told me about some of the books that he'd been working on, all of them centring around the theme of forbidden love.

'Come,' he said, leading us through the flowerbeds to sit on a patch of freshly cut grass. 'I've something I want to show you.' He slipped off his backpack and carefully took out a well-worn manuscript and a stack of unfinished drawings.

'*Chahna and Ishita*' was written on the top page and as I turned them, it became apparent that this was a story of same-sex love. The drawings were a little sloppy and rough around the edges, but his words were a thing of beauty. Chahna and Ishita were a pair of women from very different families, and their parents disapproved of their friendship. The pair ultimately fell in love, but the families did everything they could to drive a wedge between them and keep them apart. Vibhor told me then that he'd taken a lot of his inspiration from Shaleen Rakesh, a queer poet and activist living in the city.

'It's a little political, but the tides are changing here. I some-times worry about what might happen.' He talked about the growing homophobia in the country and about his worries that they'd lose the progress they'd made.

'Laws can be altered, for better or worse,' he said. 'Homo-sexuality was decriminalised a few years ago, but not everyone accepts that. So who's to say that won't change?'

'Do you really think that would happen?'

'Who can say for sure? I just know that nothing in this world is permanent.'

'They're beautifully written,' I finally said, handing the pages back to him.

'It's sometimes easier to say the things we feel on paper.' He carefully took the manuscript. 'We tell ourselves lies every day – sometimes there's more truth in fiction.'

'And Amrit? What does she think of all of this?'

'We have an understanding.' He smiled softly. 'Our marriage is one of convenience. We don't interfere in one another's busi-ness.' He lingered over the words as he said them, holding eye contact for a moment, as if making sure I'd understood. I knew that lavender marriages existed – it wasn't uncommon for gay people to disguise their identity with a heterosexual marriage – but was that really what Vibhor was referring to?

I thought on it for a moment, before giving him a slow contemplative nod.

'And are you happy?' I finally asked. 'Do you love her?'

'With all my heart,' he confirmed, and put the manuscript back into his bag.

Chapter Thirteen

It was Vibhor's day off. He was as excitable as ever, beeping the horn of his little red car as he pulled up outside the hotel. He'd offered to take me to see the Taj Mahal, and although it was an eight-hour round trip to Agra, he told me that he didn't mind. Sometimes he worked as a driver for some of his parents' wealthier clients, and he said that he enjoyed nothing more than chauffeuring them back and forth across the country.

'I got you a Thums Up,' he said happily as I climbed into the car, handing me a glass bottle filled with a syrupy cola-like liquid. I'd told him that I wanted to try it after reading about it in *Eat, Pray, Love* – my favourite book – and so he'd gone out of his way to get me one.

He'd filled the car with snacks and drinks, had a playlist of his favourite music ready to go, and he kept referring to our journey as an 'all-American road trip'.

'Seatbelt,' he reminded me as I sat down next to him. His car was air-conditioned and I was grateful for it: the weather that day was scorching. I'd barely been outside for five minutes and already my forehead was beading with sweat in the heat of the Indian sun.

I enjoyed watching the city roll by as Vibhor drove us through the streets, taking in the architecture and watching the residents busying about their lives. I'd been here for a whole week now, and aside from the implication that Vibhor wasn't entirely straight, I hadn't knowingly met or seen any other LGBT+ people. In a city of 20 million, there were bound to be countless LGBT+ people living here, but there was absolutely no visibility – there were no rainbow flags flying in the breeze, and certainly no gay couples walking through the streets. I'd opened Grindr to find endless requests for 'discreet only' and only a few faces mixed into the wall of faceless torsos. I had a burning curiosity to find out more about LGBT+ life here, and so I tentatively asked Vibhor what he knew.

He chewed over it for a moment, busy watching the roads as we sped in and out of the traffic. 'It's not something we really talk about. But it doesn't mean it isn't here.'

'Are there gay bars?'

He nodded. 'You wouldn't know it if you saw them,' he said. 'They don't really advertise themselves that way, but they're here. A few nights every week.'

'And what about Pride?' I asked, and he lit up when I said that.

'We came to watch them last year. Hundreds of people lining the streets, just here.' He gestured as we drove down the long road that sat in the shadow of India Gate. 'They had a picnic right here for all to see.'

'And people accept it?' I asked, as Vibhor turned out of the city and onto the motorway. He tilted his head from side to side in thought.

'Many of our leaders speak against it,' he said hesitantly. 'Politically and religiously. It's perhaps not something you would tell your family.'

'But do you think that will change?' I asked, as an entire family sat on a single motorbike whizzed past us, almost clipping the car in front of us as they did.

'We can only hope for a better future, but we must be grateful for the things we have today.'

I thought about that for a moment, and of all the LGBT+ people around the world who were still in the closet, or struggling. The world has certainly progressed, but it's sometimes difficult to show gratitude when you have knowledge of so much suffering.

'Do you have any gay friends, Vibhor?' I finally asked.

He shook his head. 'I have met with many strangers, but I do not have any friends.'

He said that with a hint of sadness that hung in the air between us. 'Aside from you, of course,' he added, smiling as he took his eyes off the road for just a moment.

A moment perhaps too long because we ploughed into something at full speed.

I jolted forward so hard my seatbelt felt like it was going to slice through my neck. It prevented my head from crashing through the windscreen, but as we lurched forward in the vehicle a writhing mass of limbs bounced across the bonnet and rolled over the car, spattering blood and shrieks across the motorway as it went. The force of the impact sent us into a screeching wheelspin, and Vibhor swore loudly as we were deafened by the cries of something screaming in pain.

The traffic dodged around us, sounding their horns furiously as Vibhor struggled to regain control of the vehicle. I spun round in my seat to see something lying in the middle of the road, desperately trying to crawl itself to safety. A few cars swerved out of the way but another ran into it at full pelt, silencing it with one last ungodly yelp.

'Pull over!' I yelled, but I knew there was nothing we could do.

'It's just a dog,' Vibhor said as if to himself, his hands trembling on the steering wheel. 'It's just a dog,' he repeated, trying to calm himself, and then whispered to himself in Hindi.

'It's not your fault,' I said quietly, and he nodded just as the engine began to smoke and splutter. I leaned forward and could see flecks of fresh blood spattered against the dented hood of the car. A single hairline crack ran the entire length of the windscreen. The air conditioning cut out, and the car felt like a furnace by the time Vibhor pulled us into an emergency stop a few miles down the road.

'I'm sorry,' Vibhor said. 'I'll fix this, please stay here.' He unbuckled his seatbelt and climbed out of the car. I ignored what he'd said and followed suit.

I'd only been in India for one week and I'd somehow managed to find myself stranded at the side of the motorway twice. This time, though, we weren't alone – there was a small slum lining the side of the motorway, and a group of wide-eyed children sat on one of the makeshift roofs, eyeing us in curiosity. Vibhor tried to call and beckon them over, but they just watched him with suspicion and then slunk away back into the slum.

Vibhor popped the hood up and began fussing over the bowels of the vehicle, and I noticed then that one of our headlights had been completely shattered from the impact. I tried to stand next to him so I could watch as he checked each component carefully, twiddling and twisting as he searched for the cause of the problem, but the heat from the car was so unbearable that I had to stand back.

'Anything I can do to help?' I asked. Vibhor shook his head.

'I've got this. I'll sort this,' he said, but as much as he tried to make it look like he had everything under control, it became apparent that he had no idea what he was doing. He eventually pulled out his phone and called for assistance, but was told it would be four to six hours before they could get somebody out to help us.

'We might be stuck here for a little while,' he said apologetically, and then waved his hands frantically when he spotted a fresh set of faces appearing from the slums.

'Everything okay?' a friendly stranger asked as several men came out to join us. All of them started looking over the car and discussing what might be the problem. Some of them offered solutions and even managed to procure spare parts, but none of them could fix it.

It was clear that these people didn't have very much, but there was no talk of money or favours – they all just wanted to help. They eventually brought us a pair of deckchairs to sit in and some of the women offered us water and fresh fruit as the kids began to swarm around us with their newfound confidence. They seemed particularly fascinated with me, and sat cross-legged around me as they laughed and giggled and asked me to play games with them. Vibhor distracted them with some paper and pencils from his bag and started to draw with them. All of them were so wonderfully creative and it was a pleasure to watch them work.

It reminded me of being in my classroom with my students in Italy, and having Vibhor by my side reminded me of working with Matteo. Both of them belonged to cultures that didn't allow them to outwardly explore their identity; they lived in different parts of the world under different sets of rules, but ultimately their circumstances were the same. Things hadn't been so different for Tom and me growing up in our hometown either, and it made me think of the millions of LGBT+ people around the world, and how so many of them are facing very similar struggles.

'When I was small I wanted to be an artist,' Vibhor said, as we watched the children's imaginations spilling out onto the page. 'And then I grew up and realised that I wasn't very good at it.' He laughed. 'So I found other ways to tell my stories. I still like to draw, though: it's good to reconnect with the person we wanted to be.'

'They're not so bad,' I said, as Vibhor drew an elaborate lotus with wilted petals. 'But writing is definitely your strong suit.'

'And what was your dream when you were small?' he asked.

'I think I wanted to help people,' I said, after a moment's thought. 'Or animals,' I added, recalling that long-lost dream of being a zookeeper.

'Well, what changed?' he asked, pausing to look at me.

'Life, I guess. I forgot about those dreams a long time ago.'

'It's never too late,' Vibhor said. 'You're on your way to work with animals, aren't you? And who knows what you'll go on to do after that.'

'I suppose you're right.' I smiled.

'I always am,' he joked, and placed his hand affectionately on my shoulder.

Everyone eventually gave up trying to fix the vehicle after that, and we resigned ourselves to waiting for the mechanic to come and rescue us. Some of the men brought us a couple of beers, and so we sat in our deckchairs at the side of the motorway, watching the cars hurtling by us as we waited to be rescued. It was dark by the time the mechanic finally arrived, and although he managed to fix the car in no time, we never did make it to see the Taj that day.

Vibhor lived up to his promise to take me to see it another day, however, and he was an exceptional tour guide. He told me all his favourite secret facts about the palace, and even surprised me with a detour to see the elephants in Jaipur.

'I think your younger self would have appreciated this,' he said as we marvelled at the magnificent creatures meandering over the hillside.

'I think so too, thank you Vibhor.'

It's only on reflection that I realise it was the people I'd met who had made my time in India the most memorable, whether it was seeing elephants with Vibhor, being rescued by the old man in the tuk-tuk or meeting the people who came to our aid after the accident. It was when I was with them that I felt like I'd found the real India, and in getting to know them, I felt closer to its heart.

* * *

It was my last day in India and I sat with Vibhor as we watched one final sunset over the Jama Masjid. It was one of the largest mosques in India, and with its enormous domes and winding spires, it was my favourite piece of architecture in the city. Vibhor pointed out the imperfections in its symmetrical design, and told me it was done on purpose as anything perfect in Islamic architecture is considered an affront to Allah. I liked that, and I liked that Vibhor took an interest in religions that weren't his own.

I would be leaving the next morning and so for my last meal in India we'd bought some chapatis, pakoras and dal from the nearby market, and we sipped on bottles of sugary-sweet Thums Up as we watched the silhouettes of dancing birds caught in the burnt-orange sky. Caught up in the beauty of it all, my interest was piqued by a pair of young men who were walking hand in hand down the steps of the mosque.

'Why do they hold hands like that?' I asked as they disappeared out of view.

'Because they are friends,' Vibhor said as if it were the most obvious thing in the world. 'See—'

He reached over and took my hand in his, holding it for a moment before releasing it. 'It's perfectly normal here,' he said, and I wished that were the case for my own country. Seeing open displays of compassion between male friends was a rarity, and outside of the realms of queer friendship it was something that was almost non-existent. I'd never had a friendship like that back home, and it wasn't until I left and met people like Jack, Carmen and Vibhor that I realised the value of intimacy between friends. It's considered acceptable for girls and women to hold hands and show public signs of platonic friendship, but some-how men back home are often not given the same luxury.

I believe that so much of this is rooted in an obsession with masculinity that has warped our ideas of what it means to be a man. Showing any form of emotion is often considered a sign of weakness, and we instil this into our children by teaching them from a young age that they need to 'man up' and that 'big boys don't cry.'

This can lead to us bottling up our emotions and refusing to speak our feelings out loud. Even something as simple as holding hands with a friend is somehow seen as a sign of weakness. We may consider ourselves, in the UK or in Western Europe, to be more culturally advanced in terms of acceptance, but in a lot of ways, the people of India are so far ahead of us. The thing I loved most about India was that it wasn't afraid to be kind, to show affection, and to love with a full and open heart. It's frustrating that this kindness isn't perhaps yet shared with its LGBT+ resi-dents, but it's important to remember that it was us – the British – who formally outlawed homosexuality there in the first place. It's the people of India who are working to undo our mistakes.

I asked Vibhor again about Chahna and Ishita, and if he thought that they would see their happy ending. 'It is not yet written,' he said, with a glint of hopefulness in his heart. 'But things are getting better,' he added with a smile, and I think he really believed those words to be true.

It was the spring of 2013 when I left India and little did we know it then, but homosexuality would be re-criminalised just a few short months later. The country would take an enormous step back in terms of equality, and couples who had been previously free to live and love out loud were forced to go back into the closet for fear of persecution. It was a message to the world that LGBT+ advancements are never guaranteed, just like Vibhor said – laws can be changed, for better or for worse, and that change would hold back the LGBT+ community in India for five long and painful years.

Thankfully that decision would be overturned again in 2018, decriminalising homosexuality for a second time – hopefully, this time, for good. It's certainly a cause for celebration and reflection, but it doesn't mean that the fight is won. Same-sex marriage is still outlawed at time of writing and there are still no formal legal protections in place for LGBT+ people in the country. Like Chahna and Ishita and millions of queer people all over the globe, many LGBT+ Indians are still waiting for their happy ending to come.

THAILAND

Chapter Fourteen

I thought I'd escaped India without suffering the dreaded Delhi Belly, but that last meal with Vibhor must have tipped me over the edge. As delicious as it was, my western stomach was outmatched, and the fire of India twisted and turned inside of me as I arrived in one of Thailand's peaceful riverside towns.

I was on my way to the animal sanctuary but I hadn't quite realised how remote it was. Miles away from anything, it was out in a forest temple in the middle of nowhere. The Buddhist monks who ran the place offered to feed and house me in exchange for me helping to take care of the animals, and although I knew nothing about Buddhism, I was excited to immerse myself into a whole new way of living.

It was a six-hour journey out into the countryside, and so I'd resolved to break up the journey by stopping off in a little town that sat halfway between the sanctuary and the rest of civilisation. There was just one single street that ran along the riverside, and the whole place was decorated with paper lanterns and bamboo. A few little bars opened out onto the street, their barstools teetering on the edge of the road as cars drove around them, and the only guesthouse in town sat between them. I'd phoned ahead and spoken to the owner. Her name was Lawaan, and even though it was well past midnight, she agreed to wait up for me and waved me down when I arrived.

'*Sawadee ka*,' she said, placing her hands together at her heart in the greeting known as a *wai*. Lawaan was beautiful – she wore a flowing floral dress and fresh flowers in her hair, and her personality sparkled as brightly as the rubies she wore on her wrist. She seemed immediately concerned when she saw me clutching at my stomach, and quickly offered to whip up one of her home-made remedies to fix it. I politely declined, feeling guilty for having kept her up so late already, but she insisted and sat me down at the bar, where she began mixing up a pair of drinks.

'We don't get many tourists here,' she said. 'What brings you so far out this way?'

I told her about my job in the forest temple and she instantly lit up.

'They're very nice people – they come here every weekend.'

'The monks?' I said, and she shook her head with a laugh.

'The workers. There's a few others just like you. Very very nice people.'

It was a relief to hear that. I'd been nervous about this new adventure, and knowing I wasn't going to be alone with the monks was reassuring. I'd been a little concerned about the possibility of having to hide my sexuality again, but meeting Lawaan and seeing her be so open and welcoming helped to put my mind at ease.

Lawaan was LGBT+ herself. She described herself as a *kathoey,* and was the first person I ever met who identified as such. Admittedly it wasn't something I understood until I met her – *kathoey* is a term that is usually used to describe effeminate gay men, transgender women or people of a third gender, but it's hard to define by our western understanding of what it means to be trans. In Thailand, some believe that every person's spirit contains both male and female genders, and that goes a long way towards explaining why their understanding of trans identities is different to ours, and perhaps why they have one of the largest trans communities in the world.

'It's different for every single person,' Lawaan explained. 'Some choose to identify as *kathoey*, but a lot of people don't like that. They see it as a word that's been forced upon us, that lessens who we are,' she went on, shaking up her colourful concoction. 'But as long as people are respectful, I don't really mind what they call me.'

'But are people respectful?' I asked as she tipped the contents of the shaker into a pair of glasses and finished them with an orange wedge and a pair of candy-stripe straws.

'Mostly,' she said. '*Kathoeys* are common here; we're big business here in Thailand, but that doesn't mean that we're considered equal. There's still no laws to protect us, and people still look at us and think that this is a lifestyle choice rather than a way of being. They think I can just "go back to being a boy" tomorrow, but I can't, because I never was one. This is who I am and who I've always been.'

It was surprising to hear that – I'd heard Thailand praised as one of the most LGBT+-friendly places in the world, renowned for its gender clinics and liberal approaches to queer identities – but Lawaan didn't really see it that way.

'It's a great place for tourists,' she explained. 'But it's not so great for the people that actually live here. I'm proud to run my own business because you don't see *kathoey* business owners, and you don't see us in positions of influence or power. People may come from all over the world to see the famous "*Ladyboys of Bangkok*", but they treat us as a gimmick, a novelty; they don't see us for the people we are.'

'And what about the people here, in the village?'

'Here I am loved and respected. I care for my community, and my community cares for me. But it isn't the same everywhere. There are many unkind people in this world – many who would seek to hurt us or do us wrong – but we can only focus on ourselves. I try to live as true to myself as possible. We can't let those people control us.'

She smiled and raised her glass. '*Chon gaew*,' she said, clinking it against mine.

'*Chon gaew*,' I answered and sucked down the sugary-sweet liquid.

'Crash glasses' is the literal translation of '*chon gaew*' and it was just one of the many useful phrases she taught me as we sat there. '*Tam boon, tam bàap*,' she continued. 'Good karma, bad karma,' she translated, and began to explain that many Buddhist societies believe that every positive action in life is rewarded with *tam boon*, and every negative is punished with *tam bàap*. They both contribute to your overall spiritual standing, and determine your happiness in both this life and the next.

'And how do I accumulate *tam boon*?' I asked.

'Being kind and generous with your time. Sharing with a monk, meditating, taking care of animals – these are all rich in *tam boon*. Whatever is in your past can be forgotten; the temple will be good for you.'

'But what if I don't believe? In God, in the afterlife, in any of this?'

'What is there to believe? Karma teaches us to practise kindness, to take care of the sick, elderly and homeless. It doesn't matter if you don't believe in it, because karma is everywhere: it's as real as you or me.'

'*Tam boon, tam bàap*,' I repeated, to show that I'd understood. She smiled as she watched me finish the last of my drink.

'Feeling any better?'

'A little,' I said, the pain in my stomach starting to ease off now.

'Then the karma's already working. Let's get you up to bed.'

She insisted on carrying my suitcase, her jewellery jingling noisily as she lifted it up the stairs.

'Thanks, Lawaan,' I said as she opened the door to a lavender-scented bedroom.

'You're going to need a ride in the morning, yes?' she asked. I nodded. 'Taxis don't come out this far, but you can catch a ride with the chicken man.'

'The chicken man?'

'You'll see,' she said, and with that, she winked and closed the door behind me.

Chapter Fifteen

The temple was shrouded in a thick forest and you would never have known it was there unless somebody had showed it to you first. The only way to get to the temple from the town was to hitch a two-hour ride with the elderly man who delivered the chickens, and he'd make you sit in the back with them as they squawked and flapped about noisily, shedding their feathers all over you.

The whole place was overgrown and looked like it hadn't been taken care of for decades. The walls of the sanctuary had long since had their decorations stolen, and the wooden structures were so overgrown with wild vines that it looked as if the forest was trying to reclaim them. If it wasn't for the noise of the dozens of monks and workers who lived there, you would've thought that this place had been forgotten about entirely.

I'd been expecting to be living alongside a group of old and wizened monks, but in reality the monks lived separately, in their own quarters on the north side of the forest. It was a couple of miles away from the temple and we weren't permitted to go there, but I'd often see them scurrying along the beaten path that snaked up and away from the temple.

Only one of the monks ever spoke to us. His name was Kuba Chang, and at just twenty-eight, he was the youngest. He had bulging biceps and tattoo sleeves, and his friendly, charismatic nature made him inappropriately attractive. Kuba Chang didn't take things too seriously – he always had a joke to tell, and that was even more surprising when I learned about his background. Kuba Chang hadn't always been a monk – he was once a kick-boxer, and had come here for salvation after he'd accidentally killed someone in the ring.

The marks of his past life were evident for anyone who looked close enough. He had a deep scar that ran under his left eye, callouses on his knuckles and tattoos of Harley-Davidsons and bottles of Jack Daniel's wrapped around his legs. Sometimes you'd catch a glint of sadness and regret in his eyes, but he'd wipe all that away with a smile if he ever caught you looking. Kuba Chang was a devoted Buddhist monk, but underneath all of that, there was a broken-hearted person who was no different from the rest of us.

Kuba Chang often came down to our living quarters in the evening to talk and share stories, and although we were never permitted to see them with our own eyes, he would often joke that his living quarters were so much nicer than our own. I lived in a small tree-house-like structure on the south side of the forest with a pair of thirty-somethings called Rick and Ying. Rick was a tall and rugged Australian who was in charge of running the workforce, and Ying was a small, feisty Thai girl who worked as the resident animal doctor. They'd brought me here to act as their assistant and help out in whatever way they needed; they'd had a string of assistants over the years, and I was just the latest in a long line of replacements. Ying had almost burst with excitement when she discovered that we both identified as gay, while Rick told me he desperately needed someone to have 'guy talk' with, as he'd regale me with endless stories about his failed marriage and 'bitch of an ex-wife'.

Our accommodation was simple. With no running water or electricity, we slept on the wooden floor and battled daily with the onslaught of critters and insects that would try to invade our living space. It was sweltering hot and impossible to keep cool, but there was something enjoyable about living such a simple life away from the rest of society.

The temple itself sat in a huge clearing in the middle of the forest and was the hub and heart of the sanctuary, with enormous stone steps that led up to the top of a magnificent pyramid-like structure. In the evenings it would be used for meditation, but in the mornings the monks would all gather there for breakfast. Bowls of rich Thai green curry, coconut rice and pork khao soi would be stacked high in front of us – it was certainly an adjustment to get used to eating such spicy food so early in the morning, but it was a true privilege to share food with the monks every day.

They were only allowed one meal a day and weren't permitted to prepare food themselves, so local villages took it in turns to work together to deliver a feast for them every morning. It was their way of thanking and repaying the monks for holding up the spiritual standing of their communities.

A giant golden Buddha sat at the heart of the temple with offerings of fresh flowers scattered around the base, and a huge whetstone sat next to it that carried the ten precepts of the temple – the rules that all of us had to follow as long as we were on temple grounds. Most of the rules made sense to me – no killing, no gambling, no alcohol, standard religious stuff – but some of the rules were more surprising. There was to be no sleeping in a comfortable bed, no singing or dancing, no eating after midday, and absolutely no physical contact with the opposite sex. Thankfully, Rick and Ying told me that they didn't really follow the precepts; in fact they made a habit of breaking the rules. They showed me their secret stash of smuggled alcohol and junk food. They even had a battery-powered kettle to make forbidden bowls of noodles with.

'We're fine as long as the monks don't catch us,' Rick said. 'Chang's the only one who ever comes down here anyway.' He pulled a Kit-Kat from the secret stash and tossed it to me. 'And he can be bribed with these.'

It was surprising to hear that even the monks occasionally broke the rules, and secretly breaking them became a way for the three of us to bond. My absolute favourite thing was when Ying would drive the forty-five-minute journey to the nearest petrol station and come back with grilled cheese sandwiches. They were always stone cold by the time she got back, but when we were hungry they tasted like little pieces of greasy heaven.

Life in the temple was simple, and it was easy to forget about the outside world. Without the internet or social media, the rest of the world seemed to disappear, and the only thing that mattered was taking care of each other and the animals that surrounded us.

*   *   *

Before I arrived, I'd imagined that the animals in the sanctuary would all have been separated into their own enclosures, like a zoo – but, save for a few dangerous exceptions, the animals were in fact all left to roam the forest freely. The grounds were absolutely teeming with life and I was amazed by how, in this vast and never-ending landscape, Ying knew so many of the animals by name. She'd point out Dolly the blind cow and her newborn baby, Milkdud; Priscilla, an old mountain goat who would kick violently at anyone who tried to stroke her; and Misfit, an oversized water buffalo who stomped around the grounds and charged at anyone who dared to get close. Ying told me to always stick to the many winding paths that meandered through the woodland, and to never venture into the overgrowth on my own. 'That's where the real nasties hide,' she told me, showing me a picture of an enormous python slowly choking the life out of a deer.

Ying took me to the tiger enclosure on the east side of the forest last. It was home to a few dozen Indochinese tigers. With fewer than 1,500 of them left in the wild, they were some of the most endangered animals in the world. It was an enormous privilege to be offered this chance to work with them, and despite having been here for years, Ying saw it that way too. She knew every last one of them by name.

The enclosure was thick with tropical overgrowth and Ying showed me how it was divided up into different sections; how they kept the animals separate, provided food, medical treatment and enrichment; and how they used a series of suspended walkways and tunnels to accomplish it all.

The working of the whole operation was fascinating, but the thing I found most interesting was how remarkably well the tigers camouflaged themselves. There were dozens of beasts hiding among the greenery but, unlike the rest of the forest, the whole place was perfectly still. It was hard to believe that there was anything living there at all.

'Want to meet the little ones?' Ying said as she led me through the tunnels and up into a fenced-off area. Rick was already inside and unlocked the gate to let us through.

'On your toes there, mate,' Rick said, closing the gate behind us. 'Just because they're cubs, it doesn't mean they can't hurt you.'

I couldn't see anything but he assured me that they were there, all eight of them: Universe, Mercury, Galaxy, Orion, Pluto, Apollo, Venus and Solo. At nine months old, Solo was the eldest, and although tigers are usually born into litters, she'd been born alone. Rick told me that she was his favourite, and it only took him calling her name for her to come bounding out to see him. She was enormous – much bigger than I was – and took Rick to the ground with one well-timed pounce, chuffing at him affectionately as he tried to bat away her paws.

'We try to find time to provide enrichment and play with them while they're still young,' Ying said, fussing over a smaller cub that was now trying to swipe for her bottle of milk. 'But they grow up so fast, they'll be going to live with the adults soon enough.'

'And what about—' I began, but was cut off as one of the cubs tackled me to the floor, sinking his enormous teeth into my calf as I yelped and tried to pull myself free.

'You all right there, mate?' Rick called out with amusement.

'I'm fine,' I said as the tiger released its grip, leaving my leg pouring with blood.

'He's only playing; it means he likes you,' Ying said, stroking the cub's soft and shaggy fur. 'Meet Universe,' she added, at which the tiger pricked up his ears.

'Hey, Universe,' I said, leaning down to run my hands through the warmth of his fur. He was a beast of pure muscle, and at six months old he was the second largest of the cubs. He had the most striking spiral markings underneath his left eye, and despite him having torn my leg apart, I could feel myself instantly bonding with him.

'A tiger bite on your first day? That's gotta be a new record,' Rick said, coming over to take a closer look at my leg. The flesh was torn right open and I could see several puncture marks where the teeth had ripped through the skin. 'It's gonna leave a nasty scar, but you'll be all right,' he said, jumping up again. 'You'll get used to cuts and bruises round these parts. Ying will bandage you up.'

'You should see it as a welcome reminder of what these animals are really capable of,' Ying said as she retrieved a first aid box from just outside. 'He's just a cub and he wasn't even trying to hurt you. Imagine what an adult could do.'

'Why don't you take him to see Dawaan?' Rick said as Ying began wrapping a linen bandage around my leg. He had his hands full with four playful cubs who were now charging around him in circles, falling over one another as they wrestled for his attention.

'You really think he's ready for Dawaan?' she said.

'I think it's for the best. He's gotta meet her eventually – might as well do it sooner rather than later.'

Although most of the sanctuary's tigers had been born in captivity, Ying told me, Dawaan had been rescued from poachers. They'd locked her in a cage, ready to be killed and sold on the black market, and she'd been understandably distrustful of humans ever since.

'She doesn't like anyone,' Ying said. 'But she especially doesn't like men. Let me introduce you to one of the friendlier tigers first.' She called for one of the tigers as we passed by the perimeter fence. His name was Happy, and he came bounding out from the overgrowth the moment he heard Ying's voice, chuffing happily like a giant housecat as Ying cooed and fussed him through the fence. He was four years old, and of all the tigers he was Ying's favourite.

'Happy is special,' she told me. 'Because Happy is just like us.'

'Like us how?' I asked as the giant beast lolled out his tongue.

'How do you think?' She winked. 'We tried to put him on a breeding programme but he refused to mate with anyone but Big Mek. I've raised him since he was born so I guess that makes me his mother,' she joked. 'And I'm very proud of my gay son.'

'And how do the monks feel about that? About housing a gay tiger?'

'They don't really have an issue with it but they hardly encourage it either. They see it as a curse – being gay, lesbian, *kathoey* – they see it as justice for crimes that we supposedly committed in a previous life. This is our punishment: to be different from everyone else,' she said. I thought of Lawaan then and how she believed LGBT+ people in the country weren't perhaps as equal as it appeared to some.

'And what do you believe?' I asked. Ying shrugged.

'That all of us are equal,' she said. 'Human, tiger, gay, straight – it doesn't matter, we all share this world and we have to learn to love and respect each other.'

The monks were, by all accounts, some of the most accepting people I'd ever met, and it was frustrating to hear that even they had this subliminal bias against us.

'I don't think you were a bad person in a previous life,' I finally said. 'And I don't think Happy was either,' I added, and went to reach through the fence to stroke him.

'Don't be so stupid!' Ying shouted, grabbing my hand and pulling it away. 'This is a wild animal, and Happy doesn't know you.'

I apologised, instantly realising the stupidity of what I'd done.

'Rick was right. You really do need to meet Dawaan,' she added, shaking her head.

I don't think anything could have prepared me for meeting Dawaan. Ying led me through a caged corridor and into a separate part of the enclosure. 'Stay to this side,' she instructed, holding on to my arm to keep me away from the fence. 'She's coming.'

Before I even knew what was happening, an enormous beast had leapt up against the fence and was now howling at me ferociously. She towered over me and glared at me with her teeth bared, her claws jutting out like razor-sharp knives, ready to decimate me.

'Dawaan,' Ying called soothingly. Dawaan dropped her gaze from me for a moment, looking at Ying in contemplation before hissing at her as well.

'This is a tiger,' Ying said with a serious expression. 'Don't forget that. They're wild animals, not pets or playthings. You understand? They've all got this killer instinct inside of them. If you encountered one in the wild, you'd probably already be dead.'

'But why isn't Happy like that?' I said, thinking of the over-sized, cuddly housecat.

'He is.' Ying stopped and pulled off her shirt, turning round to reveal deep, lacerated scars that ran the entire distance of her back. 'Happy did this. I left a bottle of milk in my back pocket, and he did this just to get it.'

Chapter Sixteen

One of the requirements of living in the temple was that we had to meditate with the monks. The sound of chanting would resonate across the forest at about six o'clock every evening – it was an incredibly peaceful sound, not so dissimilar to the call to prayer I'd heard in India – and that was our cue to put on our robes and head to the temple to join them. Our robes were white, to distinguish us from the monks, but they weren't something that the temple provided, so Vibhor had helped me pick them out in advance. He'd taken me to Kahn Market to get them fitted, and for that reason alone I loved them. They were made of soft white linen, perfectly cool and breezy, and were something to always remind me of him.

The monks would all be sitting on their platform facing the golden statue of Buddha in the temple, chanting with their eyes closed. The sound was so much louder here and it seemed to rise and fall as it caught the breeze of the forest canopy. It seemed like a completely different place from how it felt during breakfast time: the hustle and bustle had dissipated and everything seemed perfectly still. I always felt privileged to be there, like I'd stepped into a secret world that so few were permitted to enter.

We'd sit on the floor at the back of the temple with the other workers, and although Ying would always sit in a perfect lotus position, Rick would just slouch and lean on his hand, shutting his eyes as he waited for it to be over. I fell somewhere in between the two – I wanted to fully engage with the experience but I found it difficult to focus and sit still in the stifling heat. I don't think the monks minded either way – they were so focused on their own meditation that they never even acknowledged our presence – but it wasn't really about them; this was something I wanted to do for myself.

Although I'm a deeply non-religious person, seeing the way that both Ying and Lawaan conducted themselves made me want to be more like them. They both wholeheartedly believed in the power of karma – and that was something I wanted to harness, because each of them lived their lives with more generosity than anyone I'd ever known.

The only problem was, though, that I had no idea what I was doing. I'd expected to be given some sort of instruction on how to meditate, but Rick was absolutely no help whatsoever, and all Ying could tell me was that I needed to relax and clear my mind. I tried this for the first couple of weeks, attempting to clear my mind as I listened to the monks chanting and focused on my breathing, and sometimes I did find myself entering a calm state of relaxation; but it never lasted long, and I would always end up being distracted by my own thoughts or one of the many noises that emanated from the forest. Meditation lasted around two hours, and as much as I tried, I would always find myself bored and uncomfortable by the end of it. I'd be dripping with sweat, itchy from insect bites and sore from the effort of trying to sit up straight and maintain the perfect posture.

Meditation wasn't working for me. I'd expected it to be some transformative money-can't-buy-it experience, but instead I was beginning to understand why Rick didn't even bother any more. He'd lived here for years now, and I was already bored after just two weeks.

I eventually resolved to try to talk to Kuba Chang, to ask him for some advice. I waited around in the temple until the others were gone. He smiled when he saw me, coming over and greeting me warmly as he folded up his meditation mat.

'You really want to learn?' Chang asked, inviting me to sit with him on the temple steps looking out over the vast forest that surrounded us.

'I do, but I don't really know where to start.'

'Well, why are you here? Something must have inspired you to leave home. Why are you here, and not *there*?'

I mulled on it for a moment. It had been a while since I'd thought about the reason I'd left everything behind. I thought about how unhappy I'd been in the final days I'd spent there. I tried to relay this to Kuba Chang, and then finally gave my answer.

'I left because I wanted something better,' I said. 'Something more meaningful. To find a place and a home where I belong.'

'And do you feel like you belong here?' Chang said, pointing out across the forest.

'For now. I like Rick and Ying – they make me feel at home.'

'Then maybe home for you is in the people you surround yourself with. Find your people and you will find your way back home.'

'But how does that help with meditation?'

'Meditation is about being still and clearing the mind. You just need to learn to do that on your own,' he said, his voice now calm and soothing. 'Start with the people you love and care about: wish them well, and then put them out of your mind. Then see if you can do the same for the people you see less favourably.'

'And that's it?' I said, admittedly a little disappointed with the advice.

'That's it – but it may prove harder than you think. Come and see me once you've figured it out.'

I thought about what Chang had said to me all evening and couldn't stop conjuring up images of people I loved. There were a lot more people than I'd ever anticipated – friends, family, people I'd met on my travels, people I'd recently spoken to and people I hadn't seen in years. I thought about Ying sleeping in the next room and Lawaan over in her guesthouse. I thought about Vibhor, Jack, Carmen and Matteo, and every stranger I'd met along the way. I wished them all well – and I meant it – and yet for some reason I found myself hanging on to their memories, unable to let them go.

The problem, it seemed, was that there were so many unresolved thoughts and feelings that surrounded so many of the people I loved. It was impossible to wish them well and send them on their way when I knew that each of them was battling with their own set of injustices. They were all victims of the very societies that were supposed to protect them, and it felt incredibly apathetic to sit there and meditate and pass on empty best wishes when I knew deep down that it wouldn't do them any good.

And then there were the people I didn't want to wish well at all. Images of Colin and Giovanni's father crossed my mind; the men who'd stolen from me on my first day in India; Tom and all of those people in my life whom I'd tried so hard to push to the corners of my memory. As much as I tried to follow Chang's advice, I just found myself getting more and more worked up – if anything, my mind seemed noisier and more cluttered and I felt less calm and serene than I had to begin with.

'It's not working,' I said with frustration a few days later as Chang came and sat cross-legged with me in the centre of the temple.

'But it is. In order to silence your mind, you need to first take the time to listen.'

'I don't want to just listen. What good does that do?'

'Why?' he asked. 'What is it exactly that you're struggling with?'

'I can't just wish somebody positive thoughts when I know that they're suffering. I can't just send goodwill without doing anything to back it up.'

'Then why don't you?' he asked. 'Why don't you do something to back it up? We all have the power to make a difference. Maybe it's time you did something too.'

'But what can I do? In a world that's so corrupt and twisted?'

'Make a change here,' he said, and placed his hand on my heart. 'You're full of rage. You need to learn to let go of that if you're ever going to learn to be still.'

'But what if I don't want to let go?' I asked, my hands beginning to tremble, the anger bubbling over inside of me. 'What if I
don't want to be still? What about all the people in the world
who are doing so much evil? What about the rapists and murder-
ers and people who want to take away the rights and freedoms
of others? How does being still help with any of that?'

'This isn't about them.' Chang steadied my hands as he spoke.
'This is about you, and you need to learn to let go.'

'But what if I can't do that? What if I don't want to?'

Chang paused for a moment to think.

'We don't always have to accept the world for the way it is,' he
began, 'and sometimes a little well-placed anger is all that's
needed to start a change in motion. If you can't let go, then you
must resolve to use that anger for good.' He smiled. 'We can't all
be Buddhists. Sometimes the world needs a little anger.
Sometimes we need a little chaos.'

I couldn't help smiling too as he said that. I had a feeling this
was the kick-boxer and not the monk speaking.

'Thank you, Chang,' I said. He nodded and offered to walk
me back to my quarters, but before I could even answer we were
interrupted by a deafening scream piercing through the forest,
followed quickly by the sound of Rick's voice.

'Ying!'

Chang and I jumped to our feet and headed for the temple
steps, where we could see Rick bolting through the forest in the
distance. We followed, calling Ying's name as we sprinted after
him through the woodland.

There was a pack of enormous wild boar scuffling in the
distance, and we could see Ying desperately trying to run away

from them, tripping over the uneven ground as she stumbled through the forest. The boar were terrifying – they had fearsome curved tusks that jutted out at uneven angles, and they made horrific wheezing sounds as they bashed their skulls against each other and left carnage in their wake. Rick had warned me to stay away from them, but it wasn't until that moment that I really understood why.

'Ying!' Rick called out again as one of the boar cut her off and sent her crashing into one of the trees. Rick grabbed a branch and began thrashing it around wildly, charging towards the boar and yelling at the top of his lungs in an effort to scatter the herd. The beasts dispersed but knocked Ying to the ground as they did, leaving her lying in a motionless heap.

Chang rushed to her side. 'What were you doing out here?' he asked. Ying's forehead was bleeding, and despite the temple rule forbidding him to touch women, Chang held on to her, taking one of her hands in his and speaking to her in a soft, gentle tone.

'It's Milkdud.' Ying pointed to a clearing up ahead. 'They got Milkdud,' she repeated, her eyes now filling with tears.

Rick ran up to where Ying had indicated, but it was already too late. The calf's lifeless body lay abandoned in the clearing, and her mother was nowhere to be seen. The forest could be a ruthless place, and sometimes no amount of love and care was enough to keep the animals safe.

'I just don't understand how that's fair,' I said to Lawaan a couple of days later. It was my day off and I'd hitched a ride with the chicken man to pay her a visit. I usually came to see her on Sundays, and she always had the best room made up and ready for me.

'If karma is real,' I continued, 'then what could a newborn calf have possibly done to deserve that? It doesn't make sense. None of this makes any sense.'

'It's not supposed to,' she said, mixing up drinks for another customer. 'When has life ever made any sense? When has life ever been fair?'

'But isn't it supposed to be? Isn't that the whole point of karma? To balance out the good and the bad – to reward those who live generously, and punish those who don't?'

'This isn't really about the cow, is it?' Lawaan laughed and sat down opposite me. 'I don't think you've understood how this works. Just think about it. Has anything bad ever happened to someone that you care about?'

'Of course,' I said, without hesitation.

'And did you think that they deserved it?' I shook my head. 'Exactly,' she said. 'The world is full of challenges. It's how we react that determines who we are as people.'

'But how should I react? I don't understand what I'm supposed to do.'

'Well,' she began. 'The next time something bad happens, you can come complain to me about it, or you can get up and actually do something. Think of Yollada Suanyot, Sylvia Rivera, and Marsha P. Johnson. They went out there and demanded that people listen to them. Trans women have had to demand that for decades, nobody would've heard them otherwise, and they've changed our world for the better.'

'You're right. But it's still not perfect. For you, for trans people, for any of us.'

'Of course not,' she said. 'And that's why we still need a voice. That's why we need anger. That's why trans people are still going out into the streets and protesting, putting themselves in the line of fire for the sake of the greater good.'

'It's just frustrating,' I said. 'You hear about these awful things every day and you feel so powerless to do anything.'

'You can't solve everything. Just try to live your life generously. And stop seeking the fruits of your labour before you've even begun to sow the seeds! Treat others how you wish to be treated: it really is that simple. The rest will come with time.'

'And Milkdud?' I asked again. Lawaan sighed.

'Enough about the cow!' she said. 'I'm sure she's in a better place. You can't have life without death, and it's the way we live our lives that matters, not the way we die.'

It was a difficult pill to swallow and I still wasn't sure I believed in any of this, but the next morning, there was a surprise waiting for me back at the temple, one that helped remind me just how special life could be.

'It's time,' Ying said to me as I arrived. 'They're ready to take their first steps!'

She hadn't slept much for the past couple of weeks because three tiger cubs had been born in the sanctuary, and she'd been keeping watch over them twenty-four hours a day. Their names were Little Mek, Sam and Si, and Ying had been so protective over them that even Rick and I hadn't seen them yet. At just two weeks old, they'd been kept in a dark room to protect their developing eyes; they could barely see and were only just beginning to find their feet. Rick rarely showed his enthusiasm for anything, but even he couldn't contain his excitement as Ying unlocked the door and let the first light of the day in on them. It took a full half-hour before we saw any signs of movement, but eventually, sure enough, the tiny cubs began to make their way out into the sunlight. They looked like tired and delicate kittens as they squinted into the light, growling and chuffing at each other noisily as they slowly but surely clambered out and took their first steps into the outside world.

'You're so lucky to be here for this,' Ying said, clutching on to my arm. 'Seeing them grow up is very special. It seems like only yesterday that Happy came out of that room.'

We didn't interfere at first. We watched them slowly get their bearings, and then when Ying was certain that they were ready, she started to encourage them to run. She made delicate and gentle whooping sounds and scuffled her feet, making as much encouraging noise as possible so that the tiny cubs knew to follow her. They clearly couldn't see very well and their legs weren't yet fully developed, but they playfully and clumsily bounded after her feet anyway, making their first attempts at a run.

They didn't get very far that morning before they tired themselves out and Ying had to put them back down to rest, but after that we'd go and see them every day at sunrise, watching them grow a little more each day until they were running circles around all of us. It was an incredible thing to see and in the space of just a couple of weeks they'd gone from being the size of my palm to the size of my torso. It was exactly the kind of experience I'd hoped for when I came here – something wholesome that would remind me why this life was so wonderful.

'We lose animals here every day,' Ying said. 'Sometimes the babies are stillborn, and sometimes they get sick; but all of that just makes life even more precious. It never gets any easier to say goodbye, but new life is born here every single day.'

Chapter Seventeen

It was Priscilla who woke me on the morning of my birthday. It was just past 9 a.m. and she was standing over me, bleating noisily. It was the first time I'd been allowed to sleep past five in as long as I could remember. I groaned and tried to roll back over, but Priscilla was absolutely persistent and demanded I pay her attention.

'How has a predator not killed you yet?' I said to the old goat, stroking her shaggy coat as she tried to munch on my mosquito net. She seemed to have taken a liking to me and would often show up in my room just like that. I was also the only one she allowed to stroke her. She almost broke Rick's leg when he'd last tried it.

The others had given me the day off for my birthday, telling me I should stay on temple grounds in case of an emergency but otherwise I was free to do as I pleased. It was the first time I'd been given free rein, and so the first thing I did after coaxing Pricilla down from the tree-house was to grab a bottle of milk and head on up to see Universe.

The tiger cub and I had developed a relationship since he'd ripped apart my leg the first time we met, and as I slipped into the enclosure he came bounding out to see me, chuffing affectionately as he nuzzled into my leg. I chuffed back at him – it was something I'd felt silly doing when Ying first showed it to me, but it was amazing how well he responded to it. My leg had long since healed, but his teeth marks were now permanently scarred into my skin.

'It'll make a cool scar to show people some day, huh, Universe?' I said, fussing over the tiger as he tried to steal the bottle of milk. I knew that I wouldn't be able to spend time with him for much longer – Solo had already gone to live with the adult tigers, and I knew it would soon be Universe's time as well. Soon I'd only be able to watch him from afar and greet him from the other side of the fence.

I took out a small red envelope and opened it carefully, sitting down as Universe nuzzled into my lap. Post didn't get delivered to the temple directly but my parents had insisted on sending something anyway, so instead they'd had it delivered to Lawaan, who'd kept it safe for me and given it to me on my last visit. It was the only birthday card I received that year and it made me realise how much I missed them.

'You weren't at breakfast,' Kuba Chang said, slipping into the enclosure behind me. 'But I thought I'd find you here.' He knelt down and held out his open palms for Universe, who nuzzled into them lovingly. 'You've really bonded with this one, haven't you?' he said as he scratched behind Universe's ear. The cub groaned in satisfaction.

'He's pretty special,' I said as Universe slunk away to play with one of the others.

'And why that one in particular?'

I tapped the scar on my left leg. 'He had the balls to bite me on my first day. Gotta respect him for that.'

'I suppose you do.' Chang chuckled. 'And how is the meditation going?'

'Better,' I said. He gave me an encouraging nod and then reached into his robes to retrieve a tiny object wrapped up in a piece of dyed muslin cloth.

'This doesn't belong to me,' he said. 'We're not permitted possessions of our own. But I found this a long time ago, and I've been looking to give it a home.'

'Thank you, Chang,' I said as he passed it to me.

'*Šukhšaṇt waṇ keid*,' he said as I began to carefully unwrap the cloth. 'Happy birthday. A new year means new beginnings.'

There was a small tooth inside that he had woven into a necklace. It was one of Happy's baby teeth – Chang had found it in this very enclosure when Happy was still a cub, and he'd held on to it for all these years.

'They usually get lost in the dirt, or thrown away with the chicken bones,' Chang said. 'It's very rare to find one like this – it needs a special home.'

'Thank you, Chang,' I said, placing the necklace round my neck. '*Kap khun krup.*'

'Emergency meeting!' a voice suddenly called. It was Rick, approaching the gate frantically.

'Is everything okay?' I asked, suddenly concerned that something had happened to one of the animals again – or even Ying. Rick said nothing and maintained a look of seriousness as he led me and Chang all the way back to our living quarters. He gestured to a room where Ying was waiting, and I stepped inside tentatively, worried about what they were about to tell me. As I stepped inside I saw the flicker of tiny candles, and then the extravagant Oreo ice-cream cake that sat there waiting for me.

'Happy birthday, mate!' Rick said. 'I'm not singing, but you get the idea.'

'Make a wish,' Ying said, bringing the cake over to me. I closed my eyes, thought hard about my wish and then blew as hard as I could, taking the candles out in a single breath.

'An ice-cream cake? Really?' I laughed in amazement, impressed that they'd managed to pull this off. 'How did you even get it here without it melting?'

'Ying worked her magic,' Rick answered. 'Better not to ask questions.'

'It won't last much longer.' Ying picked up a knife and handed it to me. The cake was already starting to lose its shape. 'We gotta eat now. And don't let the monks find out,' she added, looking over at Chang, who pretended to cover his eyes.

I cut the cake and we sat and ate it in pure bliss. Living in the forest really made you appreciate home comforts, and a birthday cake had become a luxury I couldn't even fathom.

'It's not midday yet, Chang,' I said, offering him a piece of the cake. In order to give something to a monk, you had to kneel before them and offer it with both hands. It felt silly doing this with a melting slice of cake, but he took it with a nod of gratitude.

'Right, we better get back to work,' Rick said. 'But we're not finished with you yet. We're going to take you out to celebrate.'

'Into town? All three of us?' Rick, Ying and I had never left the temple at the same time before – one of us always had to stay behind.

'It's tradition.' Rick shrugged.

'And speaking of tradition . . .' Ying said and tapped her ear gently. She had a tiger's paw tattooed into the crook of her left ear. Rick pulled up his shirt to reveal an elaborate tattoo of a tiger that stretched up and around his shoulder. Some of the other workers had claw marks inked into their wrists, or tiger stripes wrapped around their legs. Everyone had a tiger tattoo to commemorate their time here, and in keeping with tradition, I'd already told them I wanted to get one too.

'Everybody does,' Ying said. 'Nobody ever leaves without getting one.'

'I think I'm gonna get these.' I took out some sketches of Universe's markings from my pocket. 'Just above my heart,' I said, tapping the left side of my chest.

'Tonight, then?' Rick said, picking up the sketches to look at them. 'Our treat?'

'Tonight it is.' I smiled as he clapped me encouragingly on the shoulder.

There was an energy of excitement in the air as we climbed the temple steps to meditate that evening. I tried to focus on my practice but I was far too eager for the night ahead to concentrate. I couldn't wait for the three of us to pile into the chicken man's truck and head into town, and I only wished that Chang could've joined us.

'Since it's your birthday,' Rick said, grinning, as we met at the temple gates, 'your only mission for tonight is to break all ten of the holy precepts.'

'What about killing?'

He swatted at an insect that landed on my arm. 'You're an accomplice to murder now, mate. That's one down and nine to go.'

Despite the fact we were headed into a town that had little more life than a couple of deserted roadside bars, we felt absolutely unstoppable that evening, like we were heading out for one of the wildest nights of our lives. 'All three of you?' Lawaan exclaimed as we hopped out of the chicken man's truck. 'It must be somebody's birthday?' She beamed.

'Have you got anyone staying tonight?' Rick asked, pulling Lawaan into a hug.

'All rooms empty.'

'Well, close up shop then,' Rick said, taking the 'Open' sign on the door and twisting it round to the side that said 'Closed'. 'We'll take all six rooms – on the condition that you come out with us.'

'Of course – whose birthday?' she asked, eyeing me and Ying in mock suspicion.

'It's mine,' I replied, and smiled as Lawaan pulled me in for an enormous hug.

'All rooms on the house!' she exclaimed, but Rick wouldn't allow it. Our wages at the temple didn't amount to much – we were paid 100 baht per day, around £3 – but the rooms were the equivalent of just a few pounds per night, and so you could book out the whole place and still have change left over from a twenty.

We threw our bags into our rooms and enjoyed the luxury of the big comfortable beds for a few moments before heading down into the town to visit the tattoo parlour first. Lawaan came with us – she was covered in vibrant tattoos herself, and although she didn't have any tiger markings, her body was decorated with symbols that represented her love of life: koi fish on her legs to represent water, snakes around her hips and wrists symbolising the earth, and birds on her upper body to represent the sky. The street-side parlour was tiny, but the tattooist let us all pile into the little room, where I took off my shirt as he prepared to ink the tiger's markings into my skin.

Rick held my hand and pulled over-the-top faces as the needle started whirring noisily. It really didn't hurt that much, but it turned out that behind Rick's macho facade and fearlessness when it came to wild animals, he was actually petrified of needles. How he'd managed to sit through getting his wraparound tattoo was beyond me.

'Did Ying ever show you her prison tattoo?' Rick asked, perhaps a little insensitively, as the tattoo artist blotted the excess ink that was seeping from my chest.

Ying had never mentioned prison, and I just couldn't imagine what she could've possibly done to land herself behind bars. She rolled up one of her ripped sleeves to show me two black tally marks on her shoulder. 'One for each year,' she added with a hint of sadness.

'It wasn't her fault.' Lawaan reached over and clutched Ying's hand in hers. 'She didn't do anything. They got the wrong person, but she held her tongue and waited out her sentence anyway. She was just trying to protect her girlfriend.'

'Drugs,' Rick interjected. 'They framed her for dealing drugs.'

'I'm so sorry,' I said.

Ying told me not to worry. 'You would've done the same.'

I wasn't sure that was true. 'What happened to your girl-friend?' I asked.

'She wasn't there when I got out. My parents won't talk to me either. That's why I came here.'

I thought about my parents then, and how they'd always been so supportive of me. I thought about the birthday card I'd opened that morning, and about how so many LGBT+ people – like Ying – can only ever dream of something as simple as receiving a card from their family on their birthday.

'You deserve so much better, Ying,' I said, and she gave me a little smile. It was astonishing how unfairly the world had treated her, and yet still she was this unrelenting source of positivity. Ying enjoyed nothing more than putting kindness out into the world; she'd dedicated her life to it even though she so rarely got it back in return.

'And what about you, Rick? How did you end up here?' He was still grasping my hand so tightly that it was starting to cut off the circulation.

'Ex-wife,' Rick said, not taking his eye off the needle. Short and sweet as always.

'All finished,' the tattoo artist finally said, blotting away the last of the ink to reveal the beautiful tiger markings that were now marked permanently onto my skin.

'You're officially one of us now.' Rick beamed, glad that the needle was gone.

We returned to the guesthouse after that to get ready for the night ahead. There was something of a home comfort in gathering around the mirror upstairs to fix our hair and make-up – we were always a mess of sweat and dirt in the temple, and it was nice to dress up and make ourselves look good again, even if only for ourselves. Rick didn't join in and went to lie down on one of the beds instead, entirely unbothered about the way he looked.

'I could lie on this bed for ever,' he said with a groan as he sank into the luxurious pillows.

'Well, that's rule number four.' Ying nodded. 'No sleeping in a comfortable bed.'

'And rule number three?' Rick replied. 'No drinking?'

'I'll open up the bar,' Lawaan said, content with the way her hair looked in the mirror, and led us all downstairs.

'So, birthday boy,' she said and began pouring out our drinks as we perched at the bar. 'You've been travelling for a year now. What was the highlight?'

'Meeting people like you,' I said. 'I didn't really know many queer people before I left. I had a boyfriend, but that was about it.'

'Well, we're glad to have you,' Ying said. 'It was just me and Lawaan having to put up with Rick's bullshit before you got here.'

'You outnumber me three to one.' Rick laughed. 'How is that fair?'

'You finally get to know what it feels like to be a minority,' Ying teased.

'Is it really that tough, though?' Rick said. 'Thailand's super-accepting, right?'

'It's complicated,' Lawaan said. 'In the big cities it's more accepted, but out here—'

'The only Pride event I ever attended had to be cancelled because protestors tried to pelt us with rocks,' Ying interjected.

'Why do we never hear about that?' Rick asked. 'Why is it never reported?'

'Because it's not good for tourism,' Lawaan said. 'Come to Thailand – gay capital of the world – come drink and party, come see the ladyboys and come get a happy ending . . .'

'But aren't Thailand leading the world on LGBT+ equality? Don't people come from all over the world for – what do you call it – gender realignment surgery?'

'People come here because it's cheap,' Lawaan replied, ignoring Rick's clumsy faux pas. 'You don't have to wait months or years to see a doctor. But just because you can come here and get a pair of designer tits, that doesn't mean you can legally change your gender. I can't legally identify as a woman.'

'You can't?' I was surprised – I didn't know that.

'No,' she said. 'I can't, and sometimes I wonder if things would be different if I lived elsewhere. I often wonder what it would feel like to be treated as a real woman.'

'But you *are* a real woman, Lawaan,' Rick said. 'You're as real as women come.'

'And what about all the girls who can't afford any of this?' She pointed to her own body. 'You think the working girls can afford expensive surgeries? You think they can afford these operations working as a waitress, or a showgirl?'

'I guess I hadn't really thought about it,' Rick said.

'I'm lucky,' Lawaan continued. 'My father left me some money. He loved me for who I was and wanted me to be happy, but so many others don't have that. Many turn to sex work even when they don't want to. It's sometimes the only choice that they have. At least the girls in your countries don't have to go through that. They're given a fighting chance.'

'It's not perfect back home either,' I said. 'There's still a lot of intolerance, a lot of people still think that it's somehow morally wrong just to be LGBT+, that all of this is a "choice", one that we're going to burn for.'

'And how is that different from the way things are here? You know what the monks think of us,' Lawaan replied.

'Not all of them,' I argued. 'I don't think they all believe that,' I said, but Lawaan looked at me, unconvinced. I thought of Chang and refused to believe that he thought that way. 'Kuba Chang,' I said. 'He knows about me and Ying.'

'It doesn't really matter.' Lawaan shrugged. 'As long as they stay over there in their stuffy little temple then they can think whatever they like. I'm going to live my life the only way I know how – and I'm not going to change that for anyone.'

'Well, we're here to break their rules tonight anyway,' Ying said.

'Now that's something we can toast to,' Rick said, raising his glass.

'*Chon gaew*,' we chorused in unison and knocked back our drinks.

Rick pulled out a deck of cards and we played a round of poker, and he even joined in with singing a drunken rendition of 'Happy Birthday' just for the sake of breaking rule number seven

– no singing or dancing. We eventually ended up in Lawaan's swimming pool, which was small and covered in algae, but the three of us dived in anyway while Lawaan stayed by the poolside and dipped her toes.

'Did you finish breaking all the rules?' she said to me as she ran her hand through the velvet of the moonlit water.

'I completely forgot we were even doing that.' I laughed. 'Singing, gambling, drinking,' I began, listing off the rules on my fingers. 'I think I'm just missing one.'

'Which one's that?' she said and I swam over to her at the poolside.

'No physical contact with the opposite sex!' I laughed and grabbed her and pulled her into the pool. Lawaan shrieked with laughter as she tried to fight me off, while Ying splashed the pair of us playfully.

'That's it, you're officially a sinner now, mate,' Rick said.

'And proud of it,' I said as Lawaan hugged me and kissed me on the cheek.

Chapter Eighteen

I was so hungover the morning after my birthday that Rick assigned me to work in the bear enclosure to keep me as far away from the monks as possible, in case they noticed my bloodshot eyes and found out we'd been drinking. The enclosure was in a shady nook just a stone's throw away from the tigers', and it was fitted with its own splash pool, tree-house and rope swing. It was home to Bubbles the baby moon bear, who was four months old and had been rescued from a car found at the side of a motorway. Her previous owners had filed down her teeth and claws in an attempt to keep her as a pet, but she must have been too much work, because they'd abandoned her by the road, leaving her to die in the heat of the midday sun.

Bubbles was a troublemaker, and trying to keep her distracted while I was cleaning her enclosure was the most difficult part of the job. She didn't like strangers, and would scamper up into her tree-house and throw her toys down at you from above, deliberately making as much of a mess as possible. I'd learned to earn her trust by bribing her with pieces of fresh fruit, and came armed that morning with large chunks of honeydew melon.

'Bubbles, *mā nì sī*,' I said, coaxing her down from her treehouse. She grunted hungrily and came running into my arms, prodding me with gratitude while I scratched behind her ear. I'd learned to communicate with the animals in Thai – it was good practice, and Ying said it would make things easier if we all stuck to one language.

I hadn't expected anything out of the ordinary to happen that morning, and so, when I suddenly heard the sound of a grumbling engine approaching, I thought it was Ying and her truck. I didn't even look up as the vehicle approached, and it wasn't until two masked men hopped out of the parked truck that I realised something was seriously wrong.

'*Lūk hīmī*,' one of them said as they began peering into the enclosure. Bubbles was in full view, but I was disguised by the overgrowth, and so I ducked down to prevent them from seeing me. '*Lūk hīmī*,' they repeated. *Bear cub*.

They were both wearing black tracksuits, their black masks covering the lower portion of their faces, and one of them was carrying an enormous pair of bolt cutters. I held my breath and tried to stay perfectly still as I watched them. They hadn't seen me yet: their eyes were firmly fixed on Bubbles, who had now stopped eating her melon and was watching them warily. I looked over to the gate – I hadn't even locked it behind me.

'Bubbles, *mā nì sī* – please come here,' I whispered as Bubbles hopped down from her bench and started tentatively moving towards the fence. '*Mā nì sī*,' I repeated, but she wasn't listening – and this time, the strangers heard me.

They started yelling as soon as they spotted me. I had no idea what they were saying, but they kept on shouting aggressively and gesturing to me wildly as they headed for the gate to the enclosure. One of them reached into their jacket, and for the briefest moment I was worried that he was about to pull out a gun.

Not knowing what else to do, I instinctively started shouting at the top of my lungs. I shouted so loud that even Bubbles retreated back into her tree-house. I'd seen Rick do it many times to scare off packs of wild animals, but I never expected it to actually work on people. Perhaps it was the surprise of it, but the pair scattered almost instantly, jumping back into their truck and speeding off into the forest just as the others came hurtling through the woods towards me. I'd never heard Rick sound so worried as he called out my name, while Ying and some of the other workers came running quickly behind him.

'Poachers,' I said. I didn't even know if it was true. 'I think they were poachers.'

'Motherfuckers,' Rick swore as he watched the vehicle disappear into the woodland. Ying just fell silent. This clearly wasn't the first time they'd had to deal with them.

We found out later that they'd rammed the main gate with their truck to get into the temple grounds, and that they'd taken a pair of binturong – also known as 'bear cats' – from one of the other enclosures. Some of the endangered deer were missing too, and we later found one lying motionless on the forest floor. It must have been hit and killed by the truck as they sped out of the temple grounds.

'A bear like Bubbles would fetch a fortune on the black market – imagine what a tiger's worth,' Ying said solemnly as she joined me in the enclosure to try to coax Bubbles down from the tree-house. 'They come here and they take and they kill, and for what?' she continued angrily, reaching out and clutching the tiger tooth that I was still wearing round my neck. 'For this. They eat the meat, turn the bone into medicine and wear the claws and teeth as trophies.'

I felt so guilty afterwards that I took the necklace off later when she wasn't looking. It might have been a gift from Kuba Chang and the tooth might have fallen out naturally, but I now felt like wearing it was somehow feeding into and supporting the trade of endangered animals.

'It's a good thing you were here, mate,' Rick said. 'I hate to think what they would have done to the poor girl if you weren't. Dirty, low-life scum.' He spat.

'It's not their fault,' Ying interjected, a pang of sadness in her voice. 'They're desperate. They have families to feed, and poaching is all they know.'

Her empathy and understanding was unwavering – she didn't hate the people that did this, but pitied them.

'I just don't see how any of these animals can ever live freely in the wild,' Rick said. 'We're supposed to be the ones protecting them and even we can't keep the poachers out.'

I think that's when I first really understood what we were doing there in the sanctuary. A lot of the animals had been born here, but many of them had also been rescued, taken from people who had wanted to maim, hurt and kill them, torture them or keep them as pets. The only reason there was even a sanctuary for us to work in was because someone had to protect them from the cruelty of humankind.

The whole thing must have shaken us because none of us really spoke again before meditation. We'd all stayed on high alert in case the poachers came back, and it was all I could think about as the chants filled the air. I thought about practising Chang's meditation technique again, but my mind remained clouded with anger. It was not the time to be still.

'I can't do this, Chang,' I said later that evening as I once again confronted my favourite monk, the anger he'd told me to harness now completely uncontainable. 'All of this is so unfair.'

'And what are you going to do about that?' he asked, but I couldn't give him an answer. There was injustice everywhere I looked – the murder of innocent animals; people being imprisoned for crimes they didn't commit, or being used as a puppet for tourism while their basic human rights were being denied. The world was cruel and unfair, and I was tired of trying to fix those problems by sitting here in the temple, cross-legged. I was lucky to be from somewhere that offered me legal protections, even though they were hard-won; I had a family that loved and cared for me, and the only reason I was in Thailand in the first place was because I benefited from all kinds of privileges that allowed me to jaunt around the world at my leisure. Ying and Lawaan didn't have the luxury of just getting up and leaving, and had no choice but to play the hand they'd been dealt. I had an enormous amount of respect for them for that, and it was in knowing them that I gained a newfound appreciation for everything that I had.

'I've been running away this whole time,' I said to Chang. 'But from what? What did I really have to run from? These problems don't even affect me.'

'But they affect people you care about,' Chang said. 'These problems are as much yours as they are anyone else's, and you have the power to change that.'

'People keep saying that, Chang. But I don't feel like I have any power at all. How am I supposed to change any of this?'

'All you can do is try,' Chang replied as I threw my hands down in exasperation.

'Try what? All of this is beyond me – nothing I can do here can make a difference. All I do is fix the fence and feed the cattle and meditate – how is that helping anyone?'

'Perhaps you should worry less about changing the world and more about showing gratitude to those who have already helped you. You speak of all these people who made you the person you are, but where are they now? You're out here in the forest alone.'

Those last few words stuck with me. It seemed unfair for Chang to say that I was alone when I had Rick, Ying and Lawaan, but at the same time, I knew deep down that they weren't going to be here for ever. We'd all move on from the temple eventually, and I wanted so much more from life than what this temple alone could offer.

I wish I had come to that conclusion entirely on my own, but it was only when Priscilla clambered into my room and tried to snatch my passport that I realised I didn't have a choice. Priscilla bleated noisily as I grabbed the passport away from her and looked through the many colourful stamps. I'd been so caught up in the experience that I didn't realise my visa had expired – I'd read the date wrong and thought I had another month, but I'd already gone one day over. I was accidentally in the country illegally.

'I've gotta leave,' I said to Rick and Ying, hurrying into the kitchen.

'What?' Rick said, his voice troubled. 'Is this about what happened yesterday? That wasn't your fault, mate – there was nothing you could've done.'

'It's not about that,' I explained. 'My visa's expired – and I can't stay here for ever anyway. I just feel like I should be doing something more with my life. It seems like a sign.'

'But you *are* doing something,' Ying said. 'These animals need you.'

'They don't need me, Ying. They need *you*. You've a kinder heart than anyone I've ever known. There's nobody more suited to this job.'

'What are you gonna do, then?' Rick asked. 'Where are you gonna go?'

'I'm going to stop running. I'm going to settle somewhere, build myself a proper home, find friends and maybe get a normal job that doesn't involve getting bitten by tigers.'

'But where?' Ying asked.

'I don't know yet. I'll figure out something.'

'Are you sure?' Ying said. 'I can drive you to the border – we can head into Myanmar and you can get a new visa there. They'll just give you a small fine and a slap on the wrist for overstaying. That will buy you some more time, and you can stay with us for at least another month.'

I thought about it for a moment, but my mind was already made up.

'I can't, Ying. I don't mean to break up the family, but I really think it's time.'

'It's all right, mate,' Rick said. I could tell he wanted to argue but he just reached out and gave me a squeeze on the shoulder. 'People come and go – we're used to it by now.'

I hadn't really thought of all the other people who must have come to stay here, the people who had lived in my room before me – I'd never even asked about them until now. I could tell that Rick was disappointed, but he wasn't going to let it show.

'When are you leaving?' he finally asked.

'As soon as possible,' I said. 'I'll catch the first available ride with the chicken man and make my way to Bangkok from there.'

'Well, I'd better get party-planning then,' Rick said, jumping up to his feet.

'It's fine, honestly!' I smiled. 'We literally just celebrated my birthday.'

'You're not getting away from us that easily.' He grinned and pulled a small bottle of whisky out of a box of cereal he'd hidden it in. 'Go say goodbye to Chang. I just need a few minutes to set things up.'

'You really don't have to—'

'It's not for you, mate,' he whispered, nodding in Ying's direction. She was fussing over a box of food, trying to distract herself as tears welled up in her eyes.

The pair of them threw one killer of a going-away party that night – you'd be amazed by what they could pull together with such limited resources – and Ying managed to hold back her tears right up until the last moment we hugged goodbye.

'You're leaving,' Chang said as I approached him at the top of the temple. 'Not entirely unexpected.' He tapped the wooden floor, inviting me to sit with him.

'How did you know?' I asked as I sat down on the cool, hard floor.

'Because that's what I've been telling you this whole time. You've been wanting to leave since you first spoke to me. You never really belonged here.'

'I'm grateful to have been here, though,' I said.

Chang nodded. 'And we're grateful to have had you. So where are you going next?'

'To see my family,' I said. 'You told me to show gratitude to the people who made me the person I am, and I haven't been to see my parents in over a year. I haven't really spent any quality time with them since they moved away. I've seen so many people rejected by their parents, and I don't think I ever realised how lucky I am to have them. Besides, I'm not really sure where else I would go.'

'So you were listening.' Chang smiled. 'I was beginning to have my doubts.'

He stood up and guided me to look out over the forest, the place I'd called my home for the last couple of months. 'Remember this,' he said. 'Whenever you're unsure, whenever you're feeling lost, remember that you can always come back here.'

'I'm not sure if I'll ever come back, Chang,' I said.

'Not like that. Distance won't keep you from us – it's all right here.' He tapped the side of his forehead. 'You've always been right here.'

'Thanks for everything, Chang.'

'Just remember everything you learned,' he said, and *wai*-ed his last goodbye.

SPAIN

Chapter Nineteen

It was the smallest Pride march I'd ever seen, but even though there were probably no more than two dozen people in attendance, they made all the noise of a crowd of five hundred. An enormous rainbow flag stretched the length of the tiny high street, and a pair of drag queens danced in circles with castanets, singing at the top of their lungs as locals peered over their balconies and squinted down in the early-afternoon sun.

The town, La Linea, was a small fishing town on the Spanish side of the Gibraltar–Spain border. It was a place where two cultures collided: stricken by poverty and a history of conflict and division, it was also full of the vivacious life that the country is so famous for. It was the first Pride they'd ever thrown, and although the sight of rainbow flags and men holding hands wasn't exactly what you'd expect to see on an average day in La Linea, the people looked on with a warm and welcoming curiosity.

Although Spain inherited the same Catholic tradition as Italy, it is by and large one of the most LGBT+-friendly countries in the world. Same-sex marriage and adoption had by then been legalised for almost a decade, and polls showed that 88 per cent of Spanish citizens were accepting of homosexuality – higher than any other country on record.

The same couldn't be said for British-owned Gibraltar, where they didn't yet have a Pride parade and same-sex marriage wouldn't be legalised for several years to come. In fact, many LGBT+ Gibraltarians had crossed the border to join the celebrations in Spain.

It was Mum's idea to go down and join the revelries; she lived with Dad just a few miles up the coast, and thought this would be the perfect way to welcome me to the country. My adventures might have taken me to Pride celebrations all over Europe, but this was the first one I'd ever attended with my parents, and there was something incredibly special about watching them get a glimpse of the community I'd come to love.

We hadn't been watching for very long when a pair of women rushed over and excitedly kissed Mum on both cheeks. They were a couple from Gibraltar who'd crossed the border for the celebrations, and they spoke rapidly in a mix of English and Spanish as they delighted in telling me that they'd heard so very much about me. They were just one of the gay couples Mum was friends with; in fact, my parents seemed to have befriended pretty much every single LGBT+ couple on the coast.

It says a lot about our relationship and how they reacted when I came out. I don't have much of a coming-out story – my parents had already moved abroad by the time I finally told them, and of course they accepted me without question. I was lucky: they'd always been open and accepting of LGBT+ people, so much so that they even took me to the gay-friendly Yumbo Centre on our family holiday to Gran Canaria when I was just eight years old. Part of me already knew that I was gay even then, and seeing my parents react so casually to the sight of men kissing and holding hands was the subtlest way for them to tell me that being gay was perfectly normal. So many parents are terrified of exposing their kids to LGBT+ people, afraid of 'turning their kids gay' – my parents never had their fear. That's something I'm grateful for to this day.

They were essentially the perfect parents, and the only real problem I ever had with them was my own pride. I never wanted to ask for help; I always wanted to do everything on my own, and I think it's why I avoided visiting them for so long. I didn't want to admit that, after everything that had happened, I needed their help and guidance, but turning up outside their house with my battered suitcase was probably the best thing I ever did.

Palm trees lined the street outside their home, a long winding road snaked down to the beach and the sky was so clear that if you stood on the south-facing balcony you could make out the northern tip of Africa in the distance. Mum practically pulled my arms off with excitement as she opened the door and hauled me inside, and their yappy Border terrier jumped up into my arms excitedly.

I've always towered over Mum – she was and is exceptionally pretty and has wavy blonde hair and an Irish accent that has faded over the years. Everyone always says we look alike, especially when we're laughing – and Mum and I are *always* laughing.

Dad is a little shorter than me, too, and doesn't look anywhere near his age: he is obsessed with cycling and fit as a fiddle, and has the kindest, most trustworthy eyes. Loyalty and honesty are the most important things in the world to him, and he's done everything in his power to instil those values in me every single day.

They were both ridiculously supportive from the moment I arrived, each of them showing it in their own way. Mum had the guest room set up and had stocked the fridge with my favourite food, while Dad was more pragmatic with his approach and offered to help me find a flat and a job. I'd become so accustomed to living life on a whim and taking work wherever I could find it that, in all honesty, it was all a little overwhelming at first.

I was there for a week before I even sat down to look for a job. It was nice to relax into the comforts of my family home, and although I'd never lived there, the shelves were still decorated with all the memories from my childhood. The same pots and pans that Mum had cooked with when I was growing up, the same family photos, the same trinkets that cluttered each and every surface.

I wasn't really interested in any of the jobs I came across, but my bank account was veering dangerously close to zero, and so I applied for anything and everything that was available. I was filling out yet another application when the doorbell suddenly rang.

I got up from the kitchen table, grateful for the distraction. I was expecting it to be the postman or the window cleaner looking for his cheque, but instead I found a tall, smiling blond boy waiting for me.

'Oh, you must be Calum?' He was wearing a loose-fitting white T-shirt, baggy grey sweatpants and a pink cap worn backwards. 'I'm a friend of your mum's. I was just in the area. I brought banana bread.'

He held up a little brown paper package.

'It's vegan – my boyfriend makes it,' he told me, peering into the house to see if anyone else was home. 'I'm Fred, but everyone calls me Freddie,' he finally said, leaning in and grabbing me into an unexpected hug. 'Your mum never shuts up about you, you know. Is she home?'

'She's out,' I said. 'How do you know her again?'

'Kyle introduced us.' He read the blank look on my face. 'Mickey's boyfriend? Does she never talk about us?' He laughed. I had no idea who any of these people were and I was a little bit jealous that my mum had more gay friends than I did. 'Sorry. Is this weird? Do you want me to go?'

'Oh God no, please come in!' I said, but it was redundant because he was already heading into the kitchen. He appeared to know his way around the house much better than I did, pulling a plate from one cupboard and a knife from the other. He seemed so comfortable you'd have thought he'd just stepped into his own home.

Freddie was beautiful like a Ken doll, his make-up always flawless and his dashing blond hair always neatly blow-dried. His cheekbones were chiselled, his eyes ocean-blue and his outfits were always perfectly coordinated. Mum had mentioned countless gay friends she'd made out here and I'd always assumed they were her age, but Freddie's was closer to mine.

'Do you want to join me and my boyfriend for dinner tonight?'

he finally asked as he finished plating up the banana bread and offered me a slice. 'It's still warm.'

I wasn't sure how Mum would feel about me stealing her friends away from her, but I didn't know anyone else here in Spain, and I wasn't about to pass up the opportunity to make a new friend, and so accepted Freddie's offer without hesitation.

'We'll pick you up at nine. Pedro is going to love you,' he said, popping the banana bread on the table before heading towards the door with a happy little skip in his step. 'Don't eat all of that at once,' he added, tapping me on the stomach as he passed. 'Save some for your mother.'

I was dressed in my favourite shirt and waiting by the window at five past nine when the boys pulled up in one of the fanciest cars I'd ever seen and started beeping their horn noisily. It was a sleek silver Tesla, custom-built and shipped over especially.

'Have fun, darling,' Mum called from the kitchen, before coming out and practically pushing me out the door. I think my parents were as relieved that I was making friends as I was. 'Tell Freddie I said thanks for the banana bread,' she said as she closed the door behind me just a little bit too eagerly. Part of me wondered if she'd set this all up.

'Oh, he's every bit as pretty as you said he was,' Pedro said as Freddie helped me into the backseat. He was Spanish but there was almost no trace of an accent in his voice. He had olive skin, slick black hair, emerald-green eyes and a painfully strong jawline. He was the definition of my type and I had to stop myself falling over my words as he reached out for a handshake, his cheeks dimpling as he introduced himself.

'Handsome, isn't he?' Freddie winked at me as I blushed – he must've noticed me gawping at Pedro, but he didn't seem to mind. I think he secretly loved that everyone fancied his boyfriend. I think that Pedro liked it too.

I relaxed into their company almost instantly. They already knew a lot about me, and asked me detailed questions about my travels as we drove.

'I can't believe what happened to you in India,' Freddie said.

'And the tigers in Thailand – your mum showed us pictures,' Pedro added. It was so very strange to have two complete strangers know so much about your life, but it was flattering and made me feel exceptionally loved to hear that Mum talked about me so often and so generously.

Freddie was from London and Pedro was from up the coast. They met when Freddie came to visit family, and quickly fell in love. They'd moved into a big three-bedroom apartment overlooking the harbour in Gibraltar; Freddie would keep the place clean and put food on the table, and make sure Pedro had a glass of red wine waiting for him when he came home from work every evening. Freddie picked up odd jobs on the side to make extra money, but Pedro worked as head of finance for one of the biggest companies in the country and his generous salary was more than enough to comfortably cover the two of them. Pedro lived and breathed money; his parents were just as wealthy and he'd often disappear with them to the Spanish polo fields on Sundays to eat steak and caviar and network with some of the most affluent people on the coast.

Freddie and Pedro were rich in money but also rich in happiness, and I was most touched by the way they looked at one another. They'd been together for years but still kept glancing over at each other with bashful little smiles – they were very much in love, and I think it was the first time I'd seen a gay couple like that.

It wasn't that I hadn't met gay couples before – I had, but the ones I met always seemed to be dysfunctional, unhappy and filled with uncertainty and doubt. Most of the couples would break up within a couple of months and my own track record with men had hardly been inspiring, and so it was refreshing to meet a healthy, functioning couple who seemed so deeply in love with each other.

Freddie turned up the radio and Pedro reached over to take his hand as they drove. I relaxed into the backseat and we drove in blissful harmony as we headed down the coast and into La Linea.

We parked the car by the beach and took the long walk through the little streets and into the centre of town. Orange trees and softly flickering lanterns lined the main square and there wasn't a tourist in sight. The whole place felt entirely unspoilt, and although the town was a little rough around the edges, it had a certain small-town charm that meant it would soon become one of my favourite places in the world.

It felt like every single resident was there in the town square that night. It was a Friday and people were crammed into the tapas bars, stood shoulder to shoulder as they struggled to find space, trying to squeeze themselves into every single corner. The noise of spirited chatter hummed in the air, and bowls of olives balanced precariously on every available surface, alongside more beer and wine than seemed sensible.

Pedro and Freddie led me into one of the heaving bars, a place called La Chimenea. It was so small that the cooks had to gather around a tiny open fire to prepare the endless plates of food, but the whole place smelled absolutely incredible. We managed to grab a table tucked away into the corner and Pedro rifled off an order in Spanish, yelling across the room. A young Spanish girl gave him a little nod and a smile as she noted it all down.

I love it when people take the liberty to order food for you – to choose the best things from the menu and be absolutely certain you will like it. Pedro was the first person who'd ever had the confidence to do that with me – and I'd be lying if I said it didn't start to stir inappropriate feelings from within me. I tried to suppress those feelings, but despite having only just met him, I could feel the familiar pangs of longing waking from within me, clouding my judgement and making me feel giddy.

A bottle of vintage Tempranillo was uncorked and tipped into our glasses. Pedro was driving, so he couldn't have any, but he seemed to take great pleasure in picking out the very best wines and having Freddie and me try them. I don't know if it was my good mood or the atmosphere, or if it was genuinely just really good wine, but I've never had a glass of wine that tasted as good as that one. The food was amazing too; dozens of small plates were brought over to our table one by one – plates of grilled veal, chorizo and morcilla soaked in chimichurri, and *gambas pil pil* drenched in so much chilli and garlic that you could smell it coming from the other side of the room. All the visits to my parents over the years had made tapas my favourite food: I loved the freedom of not having to commit to a single dish, and I loved nothing more than sharing it with fellow food lovers like Pedro and Freddie.

'You have to try this,' Freddie said, pointing to a bowl of sautéed aubergines. 'I know it's not much to look at,' he continued, swirling around the unappetising-looking grey mush, 'but it tastes absolutely divine.' He gave me a little smile as he fed it to me from his fork, and I grinned through a nod of approval. It was unfathomably delicious.

The food kept coming until we couldn't eat another bite, and with a stack of empty plates in front of us, we leaned back into our seats and watched the bar begin to empty around us.

'So I hear you were engaged?' Pedro asked. 'What happened?'

'There's not much to say,' I said, and shrugged.

'Well, how'd he treat you? Did he cook for you? Bring you flowers?'

'He was a terrible cook.' I laughed. 'And nobody has ever brought me flowers.'

'Nobody? Ever? Oh, come on, I'll buy you flowers,' he said. 'Peonies, hydrangeas – what's your poison?'

'Carnations,' I said. 'I really like blue carnations.'

'Blue carnations it is.' Pedro nodded. 'Don't worry, you'll get a bunch too,' he said, turning to Freddie and kissing him softly on the lips, their eyes lingering as they disappeared into one another for just the briefest moment.

We stayed there for hours and it was well past midnight by the time the waitress came over to collect our empty wine glasses. The boys chatted noisily with her in Spanish for a couple of minutes and, although I tried as hard as I could to catch the gist of what they were saying, I could never understand any more than a couple of words, most of them relating to food. I didn't mind, though; it was something I'd got used to by then – whether they were conversations in Italian, German or Thai, it somehow added something special, and even though I had no idea what anyone was saying, it made me feel more connected to the country I was visiting.

'*Chupito?*' Pedro finally said. The waitress gave him a little nod and went to get a bottle of caramel-coloured liquid off the shelf, which she poured into shot glasses. She poured one for herself too and the boys gave a little Spanish toast in unison.

'*Arriba, abajo, al centro y adentro,*' they said happily as they banged their glasses down.

'*Salut,*' the waitress answered, and we all swallowed the sweet liquor down in one.

I thoroughly enjoyed being in the boys' company – I loved how fun they were, but more importantly I loved how attentive they were. It felt like they were always keeping one eye on me and taking care of me, and I felt very safe and respected in their company. We'd grow ever closer over the weeks that followed, and I always looked forward to our Friday-night dinners. They'd later tell me that Friday nights used to be their date night and would joke that I was destroying their relationship.

None of us knew it then, but they had no idea how much that would turn out to be true.

Chapter Twenty

I had little else to do in my spare time, and Freddie would often pick me up in his little bright-red speedster for midday drives along the coast. He'd take me to extravagant hilltop tapas bars or for coffee in the little ports where rich yacht owners met for lunch.

The more I got to know him, the more I noticed how much he loved playing the part of the spoiled partner. He loved going out and spending his boyfriend's money, and adored nothing more than being the eye candy on Pedro's arm. If it wasn't for the adoring way he looked at Pedro, I might've guessed that was his entire motive for being in that relationship.

'You're gonna die when you hear about my new job,' Freddie said one afternoon as he picked me up for our third lunch that week. He was wearing the pair of designer sunglasses that Pedro had bought him for his birthday, and seemed full of excitement as I hopped into the car beside him.

'I'm going to be a bingo host! Can you imagine?' he exclaimed.

'Like calling numbers in a bingo hall? Do they even have those in Spain?'

'Absolutely not.' He laughed. 'It's all online – I just have to sit at home with my laptop and chat with old ladies while they play bingo.'

'And it's not sexual? It's just . . . bingo?'

'It's just bingo! You should join me – they're paying me a pretty penny to do it, and they've got some more jobs going if you want one. Then maybe you can pay for your own lunch.' He grinned, pulling his wallet out of his pocket and dangling it in front of me.

I mocked him at first, saying that my last job had involved protecting an endangered baby bear from poachers and even I thought that this was ridiculous. I really did need a job, however, and I really needed to get out of my parents' spare room, so who was I to judge?

I said yes eventually and we both started working the following week. It was hardly my dream job, and certainly not the job I'd hoped for when I pictured a life in Spain, but it was the easiest money I'd ever made. I took night shifts and got double the standard pay working from midnight to eight in the morning. You wouldn't think that people would be playing bingo in the middle of the night but hundreds of people joined me every single shift. I'd keep myself awake with far too many cups of coffee and had documentaries and episodes of *RuPaul's Drag Race* quietly playing in the background as I whiled away the little hours, chatting with complete strangers and waiting for the sun to come up.

Some people came back to see me each and every night, and Freddie and I would share gossip about our most enthusiastic bingo fans. We even got to know some of them by name, though

I don't think many of them were all that passionate about bingo. They just wanted somebody to talk to.

It only took me a couple of weeks after that to save enough money for a deposit and a month's worth of rent. Glad to get myself out of my parents' guest room, I moved into an apartment in La Linea. I liked being able to walk into Gibraltar; it was closer to Pedro and Freddie, but still close enough to my parents for me to be able to see them whenever I wanted.

The rent in La Linea was dirt cheap. I got myself a small two-bedroom flat by the sea, and it was the first time in my life I'd had a place that was entirely my own. No boyfriend, no room-mate – just a space all to myself. The street outside was always alive with fishermen making their way down to the seafront, coating sardines in salt, drying them in the heat of the sun and then selling them by the roadside – just a few euros could get you enough fish for a whole family to feast on. Kids would ride their bikes noisily and the women would hang their washing out on their balconies, having full-blown conversations with each other by yelling across the street. It was always alive with character, never dull and never quiet. I loved walking through the town in my spare time, popping in and out of the many noisy and bustling bars and coffee shops, or going for naps on the beach in the late-afternoon sun, topping up my tan as I prepared myself for yet another midnight shift of bingo.

My favourite part of the week, however, was still Friday-night dinner. Pedro was always in such a good mood when he came out of his office job, ready for the weekend, and his positivity was absolutely infectious. Everything was starting to shape up into the beginnings of a life I could be content with – I had a couple of friends, a job, an apartment, the sunshine and my family just twenty minutes down the road. There wasn't much more that I could have asked for, and so, of course, that's when things would start to go wrong.

I woke up late one afternoon to the sound of someone banging on my door. There were a few missed calls on my phone and I wondered if it was the landlord coming to collect rent again. I sleepily climbed out of bed to go see who it was.

'Who is it?' I called out as I put on a T-shirt and made my way down the corridor.

'You only have one friend, who do you think it is?' a familiar voice called back. Of course it was Freddie. 'Hello cheeky,' he said in his usual upbeat and cheery voice as I opened the door, and entered before I could invite him in.

'Okay, so,' he said, gesturing dramatically with his hands as I followed him through into the kitchen. 'I think I've finally found a proper job!' He pulled open the fridge and looked inside, then looked disappointed.

'White wine?' he asked, puzzled as to why I didn't have any. 'A marketing job came up in Pedro's office and they think I'd be perfect for it. Pedro's got me an interview – can you imagine? Me, with a proper grown-up job!'

I couldn't help but smile at his enthusiasm.

'That's amazing,' I said, genuinely happy for him. He'd never admit it, but I knew he'd been wanting something like this for ages. 'When's your interview?'

'Next week. Maybe you can help me prep for it? But first, we need to celebrate – have you got any red?' he asked, scrambling through the cupboards.

'I don't keep wine in the house. You're the first person to come over.'

'Well, you need to change that, or I won't be coming back. I'll go get some – I'll be back in a few,' he said and hurried out of the door.

Working night shifts meant that my mealtimes had been completely thrown off schedule, and so I never really knew which meal I was eating; but there was one thing I was sure of, and that was that I wasn't about to have white wine for breakfast. I needed to eat something, so I started boiling some water on the stove to make pasta. Just then my phone started ringing again. I didn't recognise the number.

'Hello?' I said, tipping the dried pasta shapes into the boiling water and opening up a jar of pesto. It was a habit I'd picked up from Jack back in Berlin – Matteo would've been disgusted.

'Is that Mr McSwiggan?' a woman asked from the other end of the phone.

'Yeah, speaking,' I said. No doubt another telemarketer.

'I've got some great news for you, it's about the job you applied for,' she continued. I didn't even know what job she was referring to – I'd completely forgotten about all the jobs I'd applied for when I first moved here, and I'd applied for so many that it was impossible to keep track.

'Oh?' I said. I allowed myself to be excited for a moment, but as she told me what the job was, everything slowly clicked into place. It was a job in Pedro's office – the one Freddie had applied for.

'I've got wine!' Freddie called out as he let himself back into my apartment. 'Something smells good – what's cooking?' he asked while the woman continued to rattle down the phone.

'I'm so sorry, I'm going to have to call you back,' I said, my eyes meeting Freddie's.

'Who's that? Is that your mum? Tell her about my job – hi, Mama McSwiggan!' he shouted into the receiver just as I hung up the phone.

I think I would've felt less guilty if it wasn't Freddie who'd helped me get back on my feet in the first place. If it hadn't been for him turning up at my door with banana bread, I wouldn't have had the job, apartment or friends that I did. A better friend might've stepped aside for him and even cheered him on because he had waited so long for something like this and deserved the job, but I didn't; I wanted the job just as much as he did, and so, perhaps selfishly, went for it anyway.

It probably would've been easier if there were other candidates, but as we awkwardly arrived in the office that morning we realised it would just be the two of us.

Freddie kept a cool and calm composure; if he felt any resentment towards me, he certainly didn't show it. 'May the best queer win,' he said, before stepping into the room for his interview.

A part of me hoped that he would get the job and not me, absolving me of the guilt I was feeling – but, of course, that didn't happen. I was offered the job on the spot, and spent the rest of the day trying to figure out how I'd tell Freddie the news.

'Hey!' Freddie said when I finally called him later that afternoon, a hint of excitement in his voice. I think he was hoping to hear that I hadn't been successful. 'Did you hear back yet?'

'Yeah, they just called me,' I lied. 'I'm so sorry, Freddie.'

'You got the job?! Oh my goodness, congratulations!'

'I don't have to take it – I can turn them down,' I said. 'You deserve it more than I do. Your degree is in marketing, for God's sake.'

'Oh, don't be daft, there's a million jobs out there for me. I'm happy for you.'

'Are you sure, Fred?' I wasn't sure if he really meant what he was saying.

''Course,' he said. He sounded sincere but I still had my doubts.

'Well, dinner's on me this week,' I said. 'We're still on for Friday?'

'Absolutely. Let's celebrate – I can't wait to spend your money!'

The job was pretty vanilla. It was your standard run-of-the-mill office job, filled with pointless meetings and phone calls and about four hundred emails a day. There was absolutely nothing out of the ordinary about it, and yet I still found it all very exciting – my job history had been so random and scattered that I now thrived on the normality of the nine-to-five.

Pedro always made my days a little bit more interesting. He sat in his own private glass-fronted office, but was still directly in my eyeline. He joked that it was probably good that I got the job because he and Freddie would've driven each other crazy if they both lived and worked together. 'I see enough of that boy at home,' he'd say, laughing.

It always amused me how serious he looked while he sat at his desk, making important phone calls and bashing out endless emails. Every now and then he'd catch me looking and would fire over an absurdly inappropriate email. Pedro was a flirt and loved making people feel uncomfortable, and messing with me seemed to have become his favourite game to play. I don't think either of us realised that our emails were being monitored until HR had to call us into their office to give us a talking-to after picking up some of our messages. They told us that this was a place of work, and that if we wanted to flirt with each other we'd have to do it on our own time.

I don't think we ever really crossed a line; I'd have happily shown Freddie any of the emails Pedro and I sent each other. It was just harmless fun to us – we were just friends being silly and playful, and that was all it was. Neither of us were ever going to act upon it.

I did feel a little guilty, however, when Freddie and I started to drift apart. With me no longer free in the daytime, we could no longer go on our little coffee dates and road trips, and I now only ever saw him at our Friday-night dinners. The distance that grew between us probably fostered a little resentment, because I had taken not only 'his' job but also our time together along with it, and to make matters worse I was now spending all of my days locked away in a building with his boyfriend. Pedro would sometimes come over to my desk and call me away for a 'meeting' or a 'smoke break', despite the fact that our jobs almost never crossed and that neither of us smoked, saying it would be a waste of sunshine to be trapped inside that office all day.

'Patagonica tonight?' Pedro asked as we left the office one Friday evening, hopping down the steps and out into the blazing afternoon sun. He'd taken his tie off and unfastened his top buttons so that his chest was showing. I couldn't help but look.

We always met at nine o'clock on Fridays. It became tradition and no matter what else was going on, we never missed it. Patagonica was my favourite restaurant: it sat in the hustle and bustle of La Linea's busiest square, and Spanish empanadas and cuts of Argentinian steak would be piled high onto the table in front of us. We'd devour it all hungrily and pick apart the gossip from the week. The boys didn't mind walking across the border to come and meet me – Gibraltar could feel a little bit like a fishbowl sometimes, and I think they were both grateful for the escape. Not having to drive meant Pedro could join us for a drink, too.

'So, I've been wondering,' Pedro said, pushing away his plate as the waitress filled up his wine glass for the fifth time. 'Would you ever have a threesome?'

'Me?' I said. 'I've tried it a few times.' I thought back to the many times that Tom and I had fooled around with other boys. 'It kind of always feels like two people having sex and one person getting in the way, though. Have you never tried it?'

'Never,' Pedro replied. 'I'd like to, though.' He grinned as Freddie rolled his eyes.

'Well, I'm not sharing you,' Freddie said, putting his arm around Pedro and holding onto him just a little bit too tightly.

'Not even with Calum?' Pedro joked, but Freddie didn't seem amused.

'He already gets enough of you in the office. I share too much of you already.'

'I'm just so proud of him.' Pedro reached across the table and took my hand as the waitress came back to top up his glass again. 'He's only been here for, what, two months? And look at him, he's already making this all work. Our little boy is all grown up.' He gave my hand an affectionate squeeze, holding eye contact with me for far longer than was appropriate.

I thanked him and smiled but caught Freddie shooting him daggers. Freddie had quit his bingo job and was still unemployed; try as he might to conceal it, I suspected he still had hard feelings about me taking the job that he wanted, and it didn't help that his boyfriend was now rubbing it in his face.

'I've been looking at a few jobs myself,' Freddie said, placing his hand next to Pedro's.

'You never mentioned it,' Pedro said, a little dismissively. He didn't take Freddie's hand but reached for his wine glass instead. Freddie withdrew, looking slightly crestfallen.

'You'll find something soon,' I said with a smile, trying to compensate for Pedro's insensitivity, and squeezed his leg under the table. 'It's only a matter of time,' I added, trying to be positive but possibly coming across more condescending than I'd intended.

'Should we get the bill?' Freddie said, not really acknowledging what I'd said as the waitress uncorked another bottle of red wine. 'It's getting late.'

'It's barely eleven.' Pedro laughed. 'I'm just getting started!' He grinned, but Freddie didn't react.

Something was clearly off. I couldn't help feeling like it had been my fault: I knew that I'd been complicit in all of this, and that my flirting with Pedro maybe really wasn't as innocent as I'd been telling myself. I still had a crush on him and was playing with fire – I think Freddie had noticed the chemistry between us and his jealousy was starting to consume him. I must have seemed like an absolute asshole and I don't blame him for feeling that way.

I excused myself to go to the bathroom to give them some time alone to talk. They were deadly silent when I came back to the table: they'd either been arguing or talking about me, or both.

'Shall we go for ice cream?' I said cheerily, trying to break the unbearable silence. It was something we often did together after dinner, but Freddie's mood didn't shift, and in fact seemed even worse than before.

'Ice cream sounds good,' Pedro said, and called the waitress over for the bill. We paid and left half a bottle of wine on the table; the alcohol clearly wasn't helping. I tried to engage with Freddie as we walked – talking to him, gossiping, attempting to make him laugh – but nothing was working.

We eventually walked through the little town in silence and sat at our usual table by the heat lamp outside one of the multiple ice-cream parlours. I remembered the first time we'd come here

– we'd all been in fits of laughter over something I don't even remember, and the mood couldn't have been any more different from now.

'I'll get your usual,' Pedro said, disappearing inside to get our ice cream.

'Are you all right, Freddie?' I finally asked a little more directly, and that's when he said all the things that had clearly been playing on his mind.

'You're sleeping together, aren't you?' he said in a hushed yet accusatory tone.

'What? No!' I answered. 'Freddie, I would never.'

'Well, he's sleeping with someone.' He glared at me in suspicion.

'Pedro would never do that to you,' I said, trying to reach for his hand.

'You're always all over each other,' he said bitterly, pulling his hand away. 'And how do you explain the condoms?'

'What condoms?' I asked, unable to honestly deny the other accusation.

'We stopped using protection years ago, but I keep finding condoms. In his drawer, in his wallet, in his car.'

His voice was starting to crack a little.

'I'm sure he's just being cautious,' I said, fumbling around for an explanation. 'I'm sure he's not actually using them.'

'So you're not sleeping with him?' he asked again, teeth still gritted.

'No, I'm not sleeping with him. I would never do that to you, Fred,' I said, just as Pedro came back with a huge smile and three overfilled ice-cream cones.

'Your favourite,' he said to Freddie as he handed him a cone of rum-and-raisin ice cream. I think it was that moment that finally broke him, and you could almost hear the sound of his heart breaking as he quietly ate his ice cream. Freddie actually liked pistachio – rum and raisin wasn't his favourite, it was mine.

Chapter Twenty-One

That would be the last Friday-night dinner we ever had together. Pedro was his usual self in the office the next day, if a little quieter than usual, but Freddie completely stopped returning my calls. I suspected that something was wrong but didn't want to press the issue, and so avoided bringing it up until Mum called to ask why Freddie was leaving.

'What?' I said down the phone. 'He's leaving?'

'He came by earlier. Said he's going back to England. You better give him a call.'

I agreed and tried calling him several times over the next couple of days, but he just wouldn't answer. I eventually had to rope Pedro into a 'smoke break' outside the office, where he finally told me the truth.

'It's been a long time coming,' he said. He seemed remarkably unfazed – either he was a very good actor, or his feelings for Freddie really had gone cold. 'I should have never let him move in with me,' he added and barely even flinched.

I wondered if I'd completely misread their whole relationship. Had all those romantic gestures really been for show?

'So what's he going to do? Is he moving out?' I asked.

'He already has.'

'I should go see him. Is he doing okay?'

'He's gone, Calum. He went back to England yesterday. He doesn't live here any more.'

It hurt to hear that my friend would leave without saying goodbye, but it was clear he didn't consider us friends any more. I'd taken his job and practically taken his boyfriend. I wouldn't want to talk to me either.

'He thought you were cheating on him,' I finally said.

'I know,' he said, looking down at his feet.

'And were you?'

'No. He was just paranoid and jealous.'

I shuffled uncomfortably. I really did consider Pedro a friend, but even though we'd grown closer, I couldn't help feeling like I had to be loyal to Freddie. He was the one who'd turned up on my doorstep, found me a job and let me into his life. I felt entirely responsible for all of this and a pang of guilt sat at the bottom of my stomach, clawing away at me.

I tried to call Freddie a few more times after that but he never answered. I wasn't even sure if he still had his Spanish number; he was gone, and I never got to say goodbye. I never even got to say sorry.

Fridays didn't feel the same without Friday-night dinner – it had been the thing I spent my whole week looking forward to. Suddenly I didn't know what to do with my time any more, and so naturally I jumped at the chance a few weeks later when Pedro asked if I wanted to get dinner with him.

We hadn't seen each other outside the office since his relationship with Freddie imploded: it somehow seemed inappropriate, all things considered, but Freddie was gone and there was no point in throwing away a perfectly good friendship.

I think Pedro and I were both a little unsure of where we stood with each other – I still had a crush on him and he probably had one on me too, but it was less clear whether or not we were prepared to cross that line. We both knew it would be disrespectful to Freddie, but I wasn't sure that either of us had the willpower to resist.

'Shall we try the new tapas place in Torreguadiaro?' I suggested, but Pedro shook his head and asked me to go over to his place instead. Despite the many months I'd been friends with him and Freddie, I'd never been to their place before.

I should've insisted that we go for tapas, but instead I found myself walking over to his place and ringing the doorbell at 9 p.m. on the dot.

'It's open,' Pedro answered from somewhere inside.

I pushed open the door into his home. He was busying himself in the kitchen, searing meat and tossing vegetables into the pan, puffs of spice and sizzling juices wafting through the air as I walked through his apartment. Pedro had expensive taste – there was a fully stocked wine rack in the centre of the room, an enormous plasma TV and surround-sound speaker system, painted canvases lining the walls and framed pictures of him on yachts or in country manor houses. There were no pictures of him and Freddie – in fact, there were no traces of Freddie at all. It was like he'd never even existed.

Pedro pondered over the wine rack for a few moments before pulling out a bottle of red and uncorking it. 'It's your favourite,' he said, examining the bottle. 'The one from La Chimenea.' He poured out two glasses and handed one of them to me. He returned to the hob and tossed the sizzling pan over the flame again, before leading me through the apartment and out onto a balcony overlooking the twinkling lights of the harbour.

He'd set up a dinner table for two, a single candle flame flickering between us, with a bunch of blue carnations as the centrepiece. The sun was just starting to set, and the boats rocked gently in the harbour, gulls flapping their wings as they soared between the sails. The air was cool against my skin, and you could hear the distant sound of chatter as people began taking their seats in the nearby portside restaurant.

Pedro had prepared seared steak served with vegetables and a rich red-wine sauce, followed by a dessert of home-made chocolate fondants that were spongy on the outside and perfectly gooey in the middle. I pretended like we were just hanging out as friends, but the fact was that it was the perfect romantic evening.

After dinner he led me into his library. I never really knew Pedro had such a passion for reading, and almost forgot myself as he ran his hand along the bookshelf, thumbing the different books before taking them out to tell me about each of them — where he was when he first read them, and why they meant so much to him. *Giovanni's Room*, *The Velvet Rage*, *The Picture of Dorian Gray*, among others.

'This one seems a little out of place,' I said, reaching for a copy of *Alice Through The Looking Glass*. The spine was crumpled and the book was falling apart.

'Twas brillig, and the slithy toves—' he began, smiling.

'—Did gyre and gimble in the wabe,' I continued. '"Jabberwocky"! My dad used to read it to me when I was little.'

'I've had this copy a while, too,' he said, gently taking the book from me, a giddy warmth washing over me as he let his hand linger over mine. 'Your dad's a pretty special guy, you know? He's so cool about the gay thing. Not everyone is so lucky.'

'What about your dad? Your parents?'

'They introduced Freddie as "my friend" to other people whenever we went to visit. They're fine with it, I guess, but they're not exactly proud.'

'And what about Freddie?' I'd been waiting for an excuse to bring him up.

'What about him? Things hadn't been right with us for a while – our relationship was over before you even got here.'

'But you seemed so happy. You guys were perfect for each other,' I said, the picture of them holding hands as we drove along the seafront burned into my mind.

'We weren't. You saw what you wanted to see, but the cracks were always there.'

I thought about the times they'd bicker and argue, Pedro letting go of Freddie's hand as they argued about something trivial. Like an old married couple, I'd always thought.

'I know he was your friend, but I'm ready to move past all of that. I was hoping you were, too.'

He slid his hand across the spines of the books to meet mine. I hesitated, but there was no point denying the spark between us. I knew it was inevitable and so let myself fall forward into him, his hands catching me as he pushed his wine-stained lips against mine. This was always going to happen, and I think he knew it the first time he ever laid eyes on me.

I woke up the next morning, Pedro's soft white duvet wrapped tightly around me, to the sound of him pottering around in the kitchen. The morning sun dappled across the harbour as he brought me a macchiato, and I lay down on his chest as he began flicking through a copy of the *Financial Times*. I closed my eyes and relaxed into him, the world still for a moment as I fantasised about the life that he could give me. It was the relationship I'd always dreamed of, the perfect fantasy romance taken from every book in his library – the one I thought was never possible. I could be his house husband, arriving on his arm to fancy events, and having a glass of wine poured out and ready for him every evening when he got home from work.

He was telling me about his investments when the sound of the oven timer pinged from the other room. 'Banana bread?' he said with a smile, hopping up and disappearing into the kitchen. I listened to him fumbling around in the cupboards, the familiar scent of the freshly baked loaf drifting in through the open doorway. 'It's vegan,' he said, coming back into the room with a pair of plates.

'I'm not really hungry,' I lied.

All of this was a glimpse of the life that I wanted, and it would've been perfect if any of it belonged to me. But I was only playing pretend, and none of this was really mine – it was Freddie's.

* * *

Pedro and I only slept together that one time. I'd learned that karma would always find its way to you eventually – *tam boon, tam bàap*, as Lawaan had taught me – and this would be no exception. Karma would visit me in the form of a nasty case of gonorrhoea. The irony was that the reason Freddie had suspected Pedro of cheating was because he'd found condoms; and yet, when Pedro and I slept together, we didn't even use them.

It was stupid of me to put myself at risk like that, but I'd trusted him and believed him when he told me he'd never cheated on Freddie. But he'd lied to me like he'd lied to Freddie – I'd talked through my sexual history with my doctor, and I hadn't had sex in India or in Thailand or with anyone else here in Spain, so it had to have come from Pedro.

I was given an injection and a course of antibiotics and advised by the doctor that I should inform the person I'd got it from, but when I called Pedro to tell him, he didn't want to listen and was adamant that I must've got it from someone else. I paced up and down all afternoon after that, moving around my apartment with unease. I aimlessly opened the fridge now and then but never actually took anything from inside. I sat and idly watched Spanish television for a while, suddenly feeling tremendously alone. I was tempted to pick up the phone and call Pedro again but I wasn't sure I trusted him, or that I even wanted to be friends with him any more.

I watched cartoons in Spanish and let the day blur away until the sun finally set and the stars appeared in the sky. I stood on my balcony and looked down into the street below, where a couple of kids were riding their bikes as a woman yelled at them from her window. I didn't know what I was doing here any more – a few weeks ago all of this had made sense, but now it all just seemed empty and pointless.

It was at that point when I realised that it's the company you keep that makes a home feel like home. Pedro and Freddie had made my time here what it was and now, without them, it didn't feel like home any more. For the first time in my travels, I allowed myself to feel something I'd been avoiding all along – sadness. I'd never mourned the life and the relationship I'd left behind, and everything until now had just been an enormous distraction.

It was a difficult thing to admit out loud, but the truth was that I didn't have any friends. Kuba Chang's words telling me I was alone resonated even more now. I'd stocked the fridge with wine for Freddie, but had nobody to share it with. I'd travelled the world and made fleeting memories and friendships with people I'd never see again, but now, at last, I was alone again once more.

Monday morning rolled around and I hadn't slept much. The long walk to the Gibraltar border seemed to drag on more than usual, the palm trees appearing grey and lifeless as they bustled in the early-morning breeze. I shuffled my feet as I walked, show-ing my passport at the border control and then walking over to the office building I was still confined to. I sat at my desk all day without doing any work, idly clicking the mouse as I read the same emails over and over again – the emails I'd sent to Pedro while trying to avoid his glances across the office.

I'd made a mess of all this.

Just a few weeks ago I had been the happiest I'd ever been, and somehow I'd managed to turn that all around into the most miserable I'd ever felt. I didn't really speak to anyone that day, and as I made my way out of the office and pushed my headphones into my ears, I felt the sadness swell inside of me. I unbuttoned my shirt and let the warmth of the afternoon sun land on my skin, but it didn't lift my spirits. I got to my front door and decided not to go inside. Instead, I went up the coast to my parents' house, back to where this had all started. I didn't tell them about what had happened with Pedro, but I think they sensed that something was off.

'Is everything okay?' Mum said that evening as she pushed open the door to the roof terrace and came outside to join me. You could see everything from up there – the enormous green valley that sloped down to the ocean, the twinkling lights of La Linea in the distance, the looming Rock of Gibraltar behind that. She was holding a piece of home-made carrot cake that she put down beside me, along with a cup of hot chocolate and marshmallows. I loved marshmallows as a kid; it was just a small thing, but it made all the difference.

'Did I ever tell you about Kuba Chang?' I said, taking a sip of the hot chocolate.

'The kick-boxing monk?' she said, her lips turning into a smile.

'The kick-boxing monk.' I nodded. 'He told me to come here, seemed to think that you and Dad could help me figure this out.'

'Figure what out?' she said, standing beside me and looking out over the sleepy houses lining the valley below us. 'You're not very happy here, are you?'

'No.' I let all my thoughts and feelings pour out of me like an avalanche. I told her about Freddie and Pedro and all the things that had led me to this moment – the confusion, the anger, the guilt and everything else. She nodded and listened to me without interruption until finally we were consumed by silence. I set down the hot chocolate.

'You know you still hold your finger, where your engagement ring used to be?' she said, and I looked down to realise I was doing just that. Two years had passed and still my finger felt bare; there was emptiness there, a hole where my life had used to be. 'Do you still miss him? Tom?'

'No, not any more,' I said, and it was the truth. 'I don't miss him, but I miss the life we had. Our apartment, my friends, my job. I don't know how to get those things back.'

She thought on that for a moment as our little Border terrier came sniffing around for scraps of carrot cake. She lifted him up and I stroked his fur.

'Do you remember when you broke your arm? When you were little?' she said. 'The fair was in town and you got so excited about the ghost train that you decided to make your own. I only took my eye off you for a minute, and then I heard the almighty crash and saw you lying at the bottom of the stairs. I hated seeing you in pain then, and I hate seeing it now, too.'

'It's just all so confusing,' I said. 'I never expected any of this – I just wanted a simple life in a simple town. How on earth did I end up here?'

'That's not true – you never wanted those things. You had the most extravagant dreams – you wanted to travel the world and live in a big city – and look at you, look at all the incredible things you've done, all the places you've been.'

'But I can't keep changing countries every ten minutes, Mum. Every time something doesn't work out, I just pack my bags and leave. What kind of a way is that to live? I can't keep doing this. I can't leave you and Dad.'

'But you're not happy here,' she said, setting the dog down and letting him scamper off back into the house. 'Me and your father love having you here, nothing makes us happier – but if it's not right for you, then maybe it's time for you to go.'

It wasn't all that hard to decide where to go next – I'd been avoiding it for all this time, but I knew it was time to finally go *back*. Not to my hometown, but back to the country where I grew up. I'd always talked about one day living in London, but I grew up on small-town ideas, and such a dream had always seemed just out of reach, like such a big and unachievable goal. But with the freedom to go anywhere, and the money I'd saved from my office job, there was truly nothing that was stopping me now.

'This is the right thing for you,' Mum said as she and Dad walked me through the airport. Her eyes were red from crying – having me living there had been a dream come true for her – but she was willing to let me go again for the sake of my own happiness. A selfless kind of love that can only come from a mother. She'd always put my dreams above her own.

'Do you have to go through just yet?' she said as we approached the gate.

'I've got a few minutes.' I smiled and set down my bag to put my arm around her.

'Do you remember the first day I dropped you at school?' she said, holding my hand in hers. 'You were so upset that you refused to let me go, you wrapped yourself around my legs and held on so tightly that it took two teachers to pull you off me. You were so distraught that you even bit me,' she said with a teary laugh. 'You couldn't spend five minutes apart from me then, and now it seems that years go by without us ever seeing you. Promise you'll come see us again soon.'

'I won't let it be that long again this time, Mum, I promise.'

'You belong in a big city,' Dad said then. 'Your talents are wasted here – you have so much more to give. Just don't be a stranger, okay son?'

'I won't.'

'It's time for you to go,' Mum said, trying to stop the tears from spilling down her cheeks.

'I promise I won't bite you this time.' I laughed and she gave me a final hug.

'*Hasta mañana*,' she said, pulling away but still squeezing my hand tightly.

Until tomorrow. We'll see you again soon.

'*Love you,*' she mouthed, and then she let me go.

LONDON

Chapter Twenty-Two

It was midsummer when I first walked down Hanson Street in search of number eight. Converted Edwardian townhouses lined the street, colourful bikes were chained to the cast-iron railings and red and yellow flowers blossomed in the window boxes. There was a bring-your-own-booze restaurant at one end of the street that was pumping out the smell of fresh seafood, and there was a pub at the other, where young professionals were spilling out into the afternoon sun for five o'clock drinks.

I'd found my new apartment online and agreed to rent it without ever having seen it, so I had no idea what to expect as I pushed open the door and stepped into a narrow stairwell. It was surprisingly dark inside, and there was a faint smell of mould – everything you'd imagine a cheap London apartment would be.

My new home was on the top floor and my suitcase tore down the side as I lugged it up the final flight of stairs, my belongings tumbling out into the stairwell as I fumbled for my key and tried to open the door. I'd taken that suitcase with me everywhere, and it had survived so much – it seemed almost serendipitous that it would decide to give up now, as if it was telling me that we'd really be staying put here after all, that we wouldn't just be hopping on the next flight out of here.

My bedroom was a tiny cupboard of a room, and it was so small that the single bed blocked the door from opening all the way and you had to squeeze your way in. I shared a grubby little kitchen and bathroom with two guys who barely ever spoke to me and there was no living room, or even anywhere to sit down to eat. The room still cost me three times that of my two-bedroom flat in Spain, but I really didn't mind, as I was in London, just a stone's throw away from Soho – and I finally felt that I was home.

The room had just one window that opened onto a rusty fire escape, and the first thing I did was push the window wide open and sit on the windowsill as I looked down at the overflowing dumpsters that filled the alleyway below. Someone was practising vocal warm-ups in one of the buildings opposite, singing arpeggios that drifted into the street as they no doubt dreamed of something bigger.

Nothing really remarkable happened that day, but I'll remember it for ever: the hoping, the dreaming and the belief that it was all possible.

I spent my first few weeks in London exploring. I'd walk around the city and watch groups of friends drinking in the park, couples kissing or holding hands, or drunk people gleefully stumbling through the streets at three in the morning. I was a little jealous of all of them – it was lonely not having any friends here, but I knew it would take time. I often went out into Soho at night to take a couple of loops around the block, the rainbow flags that fluttered on every corner always beckoning me back.

I'd sometimes go into the little Italian gelateria nearby and chat with some of the locals as I worked my way through the flavours, and it was one evening, just after getting an extra-large scoop of *nocciola*, that I finally made my first friend there in London.

She collared me about halfway up Old Compton Street, the heart of London's gay scene, and a street that she would lovingly describe as the Soho Catwalk. Her name was Varsity Vane – she was a local drag queen and she towered over me at 6' 5" in her enormous, glittering heels. Her make-up sparkled under the streetlights, her oversized baseball jersey fell down to her knees and her curly black wig tousled effortlessly at her shoulders.

'Who's the twink?' she taunted in a broad Scottish accent, placing one hand on my shoulder. 'What's your name?' she asked as a group of men giggled behind her.

'Calum,' I said, shooting out my hand for a handshake.

She took my hand and kissed it. 'And where are you headed tonight, Calum?'

'I was just getting some ice cream,' I said.

'Ice cream? It's a Thursday night, dear – what's a pretty little thing like you doing wasting his time with ice cream? G-A-Y is right there, for heaven's sake.' She gestured to the brightly lit gay club just across the street. 'Don't tell me you're one of those straight boys I've been hearing about?'

'Oh, leave her alone, Varsity,' one of the boys called from behind her.

'I'm not bothering him,' she said. 'Would you like to come with us, dear?'

'Well, that depends on where you're going.'

'JoJo's,' she answered. I looked at her blankly. 'Madame JoJo's? Where on earth are you from, little boy?'

'Not from around here,' I said.

'Well I could've guessed that. Come on, then, you're coming with us,' she insisted, taking my hand and practically dragging me down the street. Her flock of boys dutifully lapped at her heels as she swept us down towards JoJo's.

Madame JoJo's was an opulent burlesque club that had all the character and charm of a working men's club but all the glitter and sparkle of a gay bar. A performing drag queen was in the process of shutting down a heckler as we entered, and the atmosphere was electric as the air filled with rapturous laughter and applause.

Varsity took my hand so I wouldn't get lost in the crowd, and as the boys slunk off towards the bar she pulled me through a side door and led me down a couple of narrow corridors to the dressing room backstage. It was so small that you had to practically press your back against the wall to use the mirror, but there were five drag queens packed in there anyway, two of them getting dressed as the other three fussed over their make-up.

'What we got then, girls?' one of them said in a thick Cockney accent as she caught my small silhouette in Varsity's shadow. 'Another one of your twinks, Varsity?'

'Oh, stop,' she said. 'I found him on the street. Poor thing doesn't have any friends – tragic, really.'

'You need to stop bringing in these street urchins,' the larger of the drag queens said as she reached into her tights to fix her tuck. 'They can't keep seeing me in the altogether,' she added as she gestured to her exposed legs and torso. She introduced herself as Cindy and shook my hand with a little wink.

'Have you got my Diet Coke?' Varsity said to one of the queens, who picked up a can and tossed it to her. 'Splendid,' she said with a smile and rapped her fingers on the lid.

'Diet Coke?' I asked, and she tapped her nose.

'It's all part of the performance – you'll see. You can watch from the wings,' she said, and that's exactly what I did. Tucked away at the side of the stage, I waited for the queens to finish getting ready, and then watched as they stepped out one by one to deliver their performances.

I'd met a lot of drag queens in my time, but this was the first proper drag show I'd ever been to, and I think it was the first time I fully appreciated the artistry behind it. They weren't just men in wigs and make-up parading around on stage – their performances seemed so elegant and sophisticated, and they were all so very talented. One of them delivered a perfectly choreographed lip-sync, one sang opera, one did half an hour of stand-up comedy, and another pulled out a surprise saxophone mid-performance.

All of them had their own unique style and way of expressing themselves, but I think it was Varsity's performance that stood out as my favourite. She'd changed into a silky green dress with long black gloves and a pair of thigh-high leather boots, and the can of Diet Coke was now strapped to her waist in a holster. The crowd whooped noisily as the lights went down and the spotlight found her in the middle of the stage, followed by the sound of blues blasting through the speakers. 'I Just Want To Make

Love To You', by Etta James – the music from the famous Diet
Coke TV ads from the nineties.

It was a form of burlesque like I'd never seen. Varsity began
slowly, giggling coyly as she let the shoestring straps of her dress
fall from her shoulders, encouraging the audience to eat right
out of the palm of her hand. They howled like a pack of wolves
as she seductively popped a black-feathered fan and began
sensually pulling off her dress to reveal a corset and silky linge-
rie underneath. She tossed her dress into the audience and they
cheered as she teased them, delicately taking off her gloves and
beginning to unlace her corset.

And that's when she reached for the can of Coke. She ran her
tongue along its exterior, and then plunged it between her legs.
She shook the can violently, quivering with mimed ecstasy that
became more and more exaggerated – until she finally opened
the can and sprayed its contents all over her exposed body.
Dropping to her knees, she leaned towards the audience and let
the Diet Coke trickle down her abs and thighs as the crowd went
absolutely wild for her.

'That was something,' I said, impressed, as she slipped
offstage and back behind the red velvet curtain. The crowd was
still begging for an encore.

'All in a day's work, dear.'

'So this is your job then?'

'Well, I don't do it for the good of my health.' She laughed
and gave my shoulders a little squeeze. 'Come on, piggy, there's
tequila to be had.'

Varsity pulled me back into the dressing room where the girls
were already taking off their wigs and dresses and fidgeting with

the fake padding that made their bums, hips and tits. Cindy brought out a bottle of tequila and we knocked back shots with salt and lime before Varsity put on her baseball jersey and led me back out into the streets.

Varsity had absolutely nothing to gain by taking me along with her, and yet she seemed determined to take me under her wing anyway. We ducked and dived in and out of Soho's various gay bars, going through back doors and down flights of steps into hidden little venues that you'd never have known were there. There was Freedom with its greased-up stripper pole, the Shadow Lounge with its champagne on ice and the Friendly Society with its decapitated Barbie dolls precariously stuck to the ceiling. Varsity was greeted with enthusiasm in every bar we went into – everyone knew her name and gladly poured out free drinks for her, and she was kind and courteous to all of them.

There's a stereotype of drag queens as being mean, bitchy and pointed, but the drag queens I met on my travels and here in London were some of the kindest and most generous people I'd ever met. They helped me when I was at my most vulnerable and made me feel like a part of something whenever I'd felt like an outsider. Many of London's drag queens have treated me with this kindness over the years when nobody else would. They're not just the hostesses of the LGBT+ scene, but also pioneers, all champions of our community and people to whom we owe so much more than we probably realise.

Chapter Twenty-Three

Varsity introduced me to everyone that night as if I were her lifelong friend. We eventually hailed a cab to take us to Heaven, which was nearby but not close enough for Varsity to walk to in her heels. Although I'd never been there, it was a place I'd been hearing about since the day I first came out.

Heaven sat and still sits tucked away underneath the arches of Charing Cross station, and if it wasn't for the long, snaking queue of suggestively dressed men outside, I'd have never even guessed it was there. Heaven opened in 1979 and has since very much become a great British queer institution – loathe it or love it, almost every gay man I've ever met has gone through that double set of doors at some point in their lives. Its history is rich with both celebration and tragedy – older men would later tell me that it was a safe space for LGBT+ people during the HIV/AIDS epidemic. They'd say that people still flocked through its doors every week, and that there was a feeling of community that they hadn't felt before. People were afraid, but people still went there – to feel accepted, to feel loved and to feel like they belonged.

It used to be frequented by the likes of Madonna and Freddie Mercury, and today you can still find modern-day pop stars and gay icons like Gaga and Kylie gracing the stage every weekend. I've also spent many a night there dancing to LGBT+ artists like Troye Sivan, Kim Petras or MNEK.

I would come to spend countless nights there over the years that followed, but that night was the first time I'd ever set foot in there, and I was blissfully ignorant of the whole other world that descended down between those arches.

'Hang with Me' by Robyn was blasting from the open doorway when Varsity took my hand and pulled me past the long queue of people, slipping straight past the bouncer and down into the club without him even acknowledging us. If there's one thing I learned from Carmen in Ibiza, it was that drag queens didn't queue.

'Right, get yourself a drink. Mama's gotta work,' she said and disappeared through a pair of double doors. I had no idea she was going to leave me on my own, but I had enough liquid courage swirling around my stomach to attempt to make some friends.

I got myself a drink and timidly walked through one of the many arches and out onto a dance floor of thumping music. It was the biggest gay club I'd ever been in – bigger than any of the clubs I'd visited in Berlin, and certainly bigger than the tiny bar that Tom and I used to live opposite. People were packed onto the balcony overlooking the stage and the dance floor was filled with hundreds of guys, mostly in their early twenties – around the same age as I was. Everyone was so pretty and attractive that suddenly friendship had descended down my list of priorities.

I squeezed my way through the dense crowd of dancing bodies, timidly making eye contact with and smiling at a few guys who glanced in my direction, but before I could build up the confidence to say hi to any of them, the room exploded with cheering and applause as Varsity appeared on the stage with another pair of drag queens.

I'd unknowingly been taken to an event night called 'Porn Idol' – something that goes on every Thursday night to this day. It's essentially a stripping competition, where people are invited to strip on stage to their favourite music while the drag queens judge them with bottomless compliments and snarky off-handed remarks. I hadn't expected to see Varsity up there on stage – she was a mystery to me: one moment she would be on stage, and the next she would be beside you at the bar; she was always on, always in character, and she never seemed to stop working.

The first contestant stepped out onto the stage and grabbed the pole vigorously as nineties pop music blasted from the speakers. He was incredibly attractive and I'd be lying if I told you my eyes were fixed on anything else but him. The drag queens each scored him a 9 and he took a little bow as he picked up his underwear and then slunk back off the stage.

'Are you gonna go up?' a small voice said from behind me. I turned round to see a pair of blue eyes staring at me from underneath a long, curly brown fringe.

'Me?' I said, taken a little off guard as a girl got on the stage, tore her top off and threw it into the cheering crowd. 'No, I don't think so. I'd consider it if it wasn't for everyone filming it on their phones.' I gestured to all the people in the crowd who were recording every single moment of the competition.

'What's your name?' he asked. He was a little awkward in his eagerness, but I found it endearing, and I was flattered that somebody as attractive as him was taking an interest in me. I told him my name and he shook my hand as he introduced himself as Alfie. He was young, no more than twenty years old, and his eyes glinted with a spark of innocence.

'Have you been here before?' I asked.

'I come here all the time,' he said with a smile.

'It's my first time.' At that point the crowd broke into applause for the girl on stage, who was now fishing her underwear from the floor.

'I can show you around?' he offered, and then coyly reached for my hand.

'Sure,' I said.

Alfie led me back through the crowd and away from the dance floor just as I could hear the drag queens giving the girl on stage solid 10s across the board. I had thought that to be the only room in the nightclub, but Alfie led me down several passage-ways and through doors I hadn't realised were even there, show-ing me different rooms and hidden nooks where boys were engaging in some exceptionally heavy petting. He seemed to take great pleasure in sharing my first time here with me, and although he seemed shy and timid he kept making little advances, as if trying to build up the courage to make a move.

'Shall I take you up to the balcony?' he finally said, trying to lead me up another flight of stairs, but I caught his hand and stopped him.

'Let's just stay here,' I said, smiling, taking both of his hands and slowly pulling him into a kiss. His lips were soft and gentle and he sighed softly as he wrapped his arms around me. I could have stayed there kissing him for ever, but we were getting in everyone's way.

'Put down that twink, McSwiggan,' a voice suddenly boomed from behind me. I turned round to see Varsity, her lips pursed. 'How are you holding up, little one?' she said to Alfie as she greeted him with a kiss on both cheeks. She seemed very mothering towards him, and they appeared to have been friends for a while.

'I'm all good,' he said in his soft little voice.

'Didn't take you two long to sniff each other out, did it?' She winked. 'Did you watch the show?'

'A little,' I said, 'and then we got . . . distracted.'

'I'll bet you did,' she remarked, one eyebrow raised. 'Are you being honest with this one?' she said as she turned to Alfie, waggling her finger at him. 'No games this time?'

'No games,' he said, blushing, and the drag queen gave him an affectionate little flick on the forehead.

I had no idea what she meant by 'games', but I assumed it couldn't have been anything bad, and that she would've warned me if so.

'All right then,' she said. 'But I've got my eyes on the both of you,' she warned, and walked away to say hello to somebody else.

'How do you know Varsity?' I asked.

Alfie shrugged. 'How does anyone know anyone?' he said, and then leaned forward for another kiss.

'Do you wanna go?'

He gave me an excited little nod. He was one of the sweetest boys I'd ever met, but there was still something I couldn't quite put my finger on. I don't know if it was what Varsity said or the way he'd been acting, but there was something that made me feel like none of this was entirely as it seemed.

We climbed the steps of the nightclub and back out into the streets above, and it wasn't until we were under the faded street lamps and away from the dark lighting of the club that I noticed that his hair was dirty, his clothes were ripped and didn't seem to fit properly, and his shoes were tattered and falling apart. It wasn't until I asked him if we could go back to his place that the penny finally dropped: Alfie was homeless, and he didn't have anywhere he could go.

I was surprised to have found him in a nightclub of all places, but he told me it was the only place he felt welcome. He told me he didn't feel safe or comfortable in many of the homeless shelters he visited, and that he was frequently kicked out of restaurants, museums and coffee shops. Nobody ever bothered or questioned him in Heaven, on the other hand, and the bouncers had started letting him in for free. He could spend the coldest hours of the night in the safety and warmth of the club, and he'd often meet someone there who would buy him food or take him home with them.

Alfie confessed that he frequently went home with people he didn't even like, telling me that he'd once spent a week living in the penthouse suite of one of London's most expensive hotels with a guy from out of town. He'd let him order room service and spend whatever he wanted, and then dropped him right back on the streets after he'd finished fucking him.

'Once you've spent a few nights sleeping rough,' he said, 'you'll be happy to share a bed with just about anyone.' He told me that he never charged for the pleasure of his company, but that some guys insisted on giving him cash anyway. I reached out to hold his hand as he said this – I didn't want him to think that I wanted to take advantage of him, or that I thought any less of him.

We got some food on the walk back to my place. He tried to pay with some of the loose cash he had stuffed into his pocket, but of course I didn't let him. I really didn't understand how such a sweet guy could wind up on the streets and I wanted to pry further, but it didn't seem like the right time. He was shivering as we walked, and I just wanted to get him home. He seemed like a smart and kind person, and I couldn't help but think of the thousands of people just like him all over the country.

I tried to push his homelessness to the back of my mind as we walked up the steps to my front door and I let him inside, but it was all I could think of as I pulled him in close and down onto my bed, running my fingers through his hair as we kissed. He pulled his coat off and emptied the contents of his pockets onto my bedside table – a couple of £20 notes, a handful of change, his passport, a phone and a charger, a couple of condoms and a packet of unfamiliar-looking medication.

'What's that for?' I blustered inappropriately, my curiosity getting the better of me.

'It's my HIV meds,' he said. 'I'm positive – I probably should've mentioned.'

'Oh,' I said, trying to hide my surprise.

'I'm undetectable though, don't worry.'

I smiled and nodded, but at that point in time I had absolutely no idea what that meant. All I'd ever known about HIV/AIDS was a terrifying, decades-old black-and-white advert that depicted tombstones and the Grim Reaper. I'd asked Dad about it as a teenager and he'd described it as a horrifying disease that would result in a slow and painful death.

I'd later learn that being undetectable meant that Alfie was in fact perfectly healthy and couldn't pass the virus on to anyone else, but back then I was clueless and genuinely thought he was either contagious, sick or dying. I think I probably overcompensated slightly because I kissed him even more passionately then, pinning him down as I took off his T-shirt and began kissing his slender body. I didn't want him to see that I was panicking inside, overthinking everything and worrying about what might happen. I remember feeling worried even as I pulled off his underwear. I really wanted him, really desired him – but I was so afraid as I touched him.

I don't know why I didn't stop him and ask him a few questions – my fear and ignorance then meant that I didn't enjoy a second of it. I just wanted it to be over.

'Does it bother you?' Alfie said as he tugged my sheets over his naked body, staring up at me with his sad ocean-blue eyes.

'I've just never known anyone with HIV before. I didn't know you were sick.'

'I'm not sick,' he said firmly. 'That's why I take my meds.' I could tell by his tone that he'd had this conversation countless times before.

'And how did you . . .' I trailed off.

'Sex,' he said bluntly. 'I had sex.'

'With who though?' I asked, and only realised what an insensitive question that was when his tone immediately changed.

'Does it matter?'

'No,' I said. 'I'm sorry, I just—'

'You just what?' he snapped. 'It was my first time, a guy from school. We used a condom but it split. I didn't think it would be a problem.'

'And then?' I pressed.

'I got HIV,' he said. 'My parents threw me out when I told them.'

'Because you were HIV positive?'

'Because I was gay,' he said.

A quarter of homeless youth in the UK are LGBT+, and the majority of those, like Alfie, found themselves in that situation after being disowned by their parents. I was lucky to have been wholeheartedly accepted by my family, and yet I'd spent my teenage years running from the home they so lovingly provided, while other gay kids were out there on the streets because they had nowhere else to go. It was difficult to admit this, and there was a certain degree of guilt in knowing I'd taken everything I had for granted.

I told Alfie that he could stay with me for a couple of days, and started researching some shelters and support services that help homeless individuals get back on their feet. He told me not to bother, that he didn't need some white knight to come in and save him, that he'd already jumped through all the hoops and that it was an enormous waste of time. He told me he was better off on his own and, when I went out to get us some food the next morning, I came back to find that he'd already gone.

Chapter Twenty-Four

Same-sex marriage had just been legalised. It was a momentous step forward for the UK and I'd joined Varsity in her West London flat to celebrate, drinking champagne out of red plastic cups and listening to George Michael as we toasted to the future of thousands of happy same-sex couples.

'And here's to all those that get divorced after the first three months,' Varsity said, sloshing an extra glug into our cups and downing hers in one. She lived above a gay club called West 5 and told me that the rent was cheap because of the racket they made downstairs. What they hadn't accounted for, though, was the racket she'd make up here.

'They've come up here on more than one occasion asking *us* to keep the noise down,' she'd cackle over the sound of the thumping music below. 'I like to be petty and wear my big platform shoes and stomp stomp stomp.' She giggled and stamped her feet. 'It does rile them so, you should see the angry little vein in the landlord's wee head.'

'Have you heard anything from Alfie lately?' I asked, leaning against the counter. We'd both see him around the gay scene sometimes but he'd not shown his face in a while.

'What, dear?' she said, opening the fridge to look for another bottle.

'Alfie – have you seen him lately?'

'Not in a while, dear; he's a clever boy, he'll land back on his feet.'

'And that's it?'

'That's it,' she said with a shrug. 'It's not your job to take care of every boy who's thrown in your direction. And it's certainly not mine. He'll show up in Heaven one of these days, he always does.' Varsity finished her drink and went to do one final check of her make-up. 'Are you ready?'

'I was ready forty-five minutes ago,' I said. 'You're the one who's taking ages.'

'Are you wearing a wig, dear?'

'No?'

'Make-up? A dress? High heels? Jewellery of any kind?'

'No—'

'Then shut your fat face and call us a taxi,' she said, coming back into the room and playfully slapping me on the cheek. It didn't take long for the taxi to arrive and the poor guy had to wait for fifteen minutes before we finally climbed into the back of his cab. We were heading back into Soho and while it didn't make much sense for me to come all the way out here just to head back into town, I really enjoyed getting ready with Varsity. I loved watching her gluing down her eyebrows and painstakingly applying her make-up; rummaging through her box of costume jewellery and her wardrobe of outfits she'd pinched from various friends; and then the moment the look would all come together as she finally secured her wig.

She was taking me to a private party in some banker's swanky apartment and, although we arrived about four hours late, Varsity looked at her non-existent watch and insisted we were right on time.

'A wizard is never late,' she said, opening the door without even knocking. 'She arrives precisely when she means to.'

Varsity sashayed through the open doorway like she owned the place and I followed her straight through into the open-plan kitchen. Loud music was blasting from the speaker system and the room was filled with people who barely even acknowledged our arrival. There were open bottles of champagne everywhere and half-empty glasses littered every surface. Varsity grabbed a bottle of vodka off the side and started pouring out drinks.

'Shouldn't we say hi to the host first?' I asked.

'If you can find him, dear,' she said. 'He's probably elbow-deep by now.' She looked at her non-existent watch a second time and handed me one of the drinks.

I looked around the room to see if there was anyone I recognised. Somebody was cutting lines of cocaine on the glass coffee table; a couple of shirtless guys were playing strip Twister; and a few others had spilled out onto the balcony, where they were drunkenly yelling vulgarities at innocent bystanders below.

'So what's the special occasion?' I asked Varsity.

'I don't know, it's Friday?' She shrugged. 'It's like this every weekend.' She gestured vaguely to the various antics going on around the room just as another glamorously dressed drag queen came down the stairs. Her name was Ebony, she had a Texan accent and she was Varsity's oldest friend.

'Oh God, not this old tramp,' Varsity said loudly as the drag queen approached us.

'Oh, Varsity!' Ebony shot back. 'You've aged terribly since I last saw you. It must have been, what, two, maybe three days, perhaps?'

'You're not looking so great yourself.' Varsity grinned. 'You've had a hard life, haven't you, dear?' she said as they embraced.

'And you are?' Ebony turned to me, wrapping her jewelled hands around mine and kissing me on both cheeks. 'Varsity's twink of the month, are you?'

'I'm Calum,' I said with a laugh, but she didn't hold my attention for much longer because a familiar face stumbled into the room. It was Alfie; he was wearing nicer clothes now, and was accompanied by a much older man.

'Alfie,' I called out. Varsity turned her head.

'Leave him be, dear,' she warned, looking a little worried.

'I should go say hey, see if he's okay,' I argued, but Varsity shook her head.

'Look, he's smiling. He's happy – just let him be,' she insisted.

'I just wish we could help him.'

'He's not our responsibility—'

'You keep saying that,' I interrupted her in frustration. 'But a boy like that living on the streets *is* our responsibility – he's all of our responsibility.'

Varsity just gave me a little sympathetic smile and shrugged her shoulders helplessly. 'I'm going to make us some more drinks,' she said and began busying herself with the bottles of spirits.

'She acts like she doesn't care,' Ebony said. 'But I've seen her slip twenties to boys like that on more than one occasion. She has a soft spot underneath all of that three-dollar make-up. You know she had nowhere to live when she first moved here herself?'

I never knew that about Varsity – she rarely opened up about her personal life, and sometimes it was hard to see that there was vulnerability buried beneath all of her make-up.

'I just wish there was a way to help,' I said to Varsity as she finished mixing our drinks.

'I know, lemondrop,' she said softly and gave me a little hug. 'But there's not a great deal we can do at 10.30 p.m. on a Friday now, is there?'

'It's almost midnight,' Ebony interrupted and Varsity tapped her imaginary watch again, as if insisting that it must be broken.

'Shall we venture upstairs then?' Varsity finally said. I reluctantly followed the pair of them up the spiral staircase, glancing back at Alfie as we went.

There were people everywhere and I still had no idea whose house we were in. We passed by a bedroom where two guys were having sex with the door wide open and I wondered if one of them was in fact our host for the evening, but honestly it could've been anyone. I never did find out whose house we were in – I never even got his name.

The apartment was spread over four floors. We climbed the spiral staircase to the top floor, where people were loitering on the landing, chatting and gossiping and pawing at each other. They didn't move as we reached the top of the stairs and we had to climb over them to make our way through into the master bedroom.

'Are you sure we're supposed to be in here?' I asked. Varsity threw me a look to tell me to be quiet. As much as she liked me, I could tell that she regularly tired of my goody-goody antics. She opened the door to the en-suite bathroom, checked to make sure there was nobody there and then ushered us both inside.

I should've known what we were doing, but I was still fairly naïve to the reality of what really went on at these parties. Varsity pulled the door shut behind us and Ebony procured a small blue rock from her bra, tipped it out onto the lid of the toilet and began very carefully crushing it with her credit card. She expertly used one of her long, sparkling fingernails to tip the now-crushed powder into a tiny little plastic bag, and then, with a lick of her little finger, plunged into the bag and rubbed some of the mixture into her gums. She passed the bag to Varsity, who did the same and then Ebony very tentatively offered the bag to me.

'Do you want some, sweetheart?' she offered, looking to Varsity for approval. I looked at the bag but wasn't sure.

'What is it?' I asked. She told me that it was MDMA.

'I've only tried it once before,' I said, 'in Ibiza. Are you sure it's safe?'

'It's as safe as it can be,' Ebony said.

'Sure, okay,' I said. 'I'll try it.'

'Jolly good,' Varsity said with a grin and Ebony offered me the bag. 'Now only take a little, it's not sherbet,' Varsity said as I very carefully licked my little finger and dabbed some of the powder onto my gums.

It was a different experience from Ibiza. This time, everything felt a lot more calm and, although I still felt those same over-whelming warm and fuzzy feelings of love for everyone around me, it was a lot more mellow and didn't seem quite as intense. We went back downstairs to the kitchen, where we spotted Alfie kissing the older gentleman out on the balcony.

I didn't mind so much any more – I was having a wonderful time, and all those worries seemed to have completely disappeared. I vaguely remember getting involved in a game of strip Twister and there was a Russian boy who was kissing me at one point, but mostly I just remember lying upstairs on the giant fluffy bed with Varsity and Ebony. We talked and giggled and shared secrets as we affectionately stroked one another's faces in our drug-addled stupor.

I know doing drugs in a suspected millionaire's bathroom wasn't the most responsible thing we could've been doing, but it felt nice to let go, to stop worrying and to just live and enjoy the moment.

'I really love you guys,' I said, taking both of their hands in mine as we lay together on the massive four-poster bed. I could feel myself starting to come down, the real world slowly making its way back to me, but I didn't mind: I'd already had enough, and reality wasn't all that bad any more. In fact, it was pretty great.

The thing that always surprised me was how quickly time seemed to pass on drugs. Varsity was absolutely horrified when she checked her imaginary watch to discover it was a great deal later than she'd thought.

'I need to pick up the kids,' she said in a fake panic, jumping up from the bed and helping us both to our feet. 'I keep forgetting to feed them and child services have threatened to take them away!' she continued as Ebony and I broke into a laugh.

The moment didn't last long as the sound of an almighty crash interrupted our laughter. The three of us hurried out onto the landing, where we could see Alfie stumbling through the hallway downstairs in his underwear, completely by himself.

'Oh God, not again,' Varsity gasped. 'Alfie, dear?' she called out, pushing past me and making her way down the steps, surprisingly quick in her oversized heels. 'Alfie, are you okay?' she called out again as he clung to the doorway and didn't answer.

I was still hurrying down the steps with Ebony when Alfie suddenly fell backwards, head-first against the floor.

'Alfie, it's Mark,' Varsity said. I had never heard her use her real name before. 'Can you hear me, Alfie?' she asked again, rushing to his side and lifting up his head. He didn't seem at all lucid – his eyes were rolling around in his skull like a pair of eight balls, and he was gurning so badly that his jaw seemed to have dislocated from the rest of his body.

'Alfie, if you don't answer me right now, I'm going to have to call an ambulance.' Varsity repeated what she'd said a second time, but he still didn't respond.

'Call them,' she said to Ebony, who immediately began to punch the emergency number into her phone.

'No,' Alfie grumbled, his eyes focusing on me for a moment before he started spluttering and throwing up all over himself. Varsity's dress was covered in vomit but she didn't flinch, letting the boy throw up all over her as his frail body trembled. She gently rolled him onto his side so that he wouldn't choke.

'Should I still call the ambulance?' Ebony asked. Varsity nodded.

'Don't,' Alfie mumbled again, his voice frail.

'What have you taken, dear?' Varsity said, but when Alfie refused to answer she took over and phoned the ambulance herself. 'I'm so sorry, Alfie,' she whispered, clutching his trembling body. 'You don't deserve any of this.'

'Is there anything we can do?' I asked softly. I'd never seen anyone have such a bad reaction to drugs before, and I felt entirely unable to help.

'No,' Varsity said. 'I've got this. Ebony, would you take Calum home?'

Ebony nodded, taking my hand in hers. All of this had been so at odds with the experience I'd had taking drugs so far – I'd willingly turned a blind eye to what drugs can do to a person – but now I was confronted with the reality and it was impossible to ignore.

There's an enormous problem with substance abuse within our community, and this goes hand in hand with many of the mental health issues that we're disproportionately affected by. Depression, anxiety, suicidal thoughts – these are all things that LGBT+ people experience at a much higher rate, and they all increase the risk of substance abuse. Combine this with the fact that drugs are so readily available in LGBT+ spaces, and you have the recipe for an epidemic that has affected our community for decades. Gay men in particular are putting themselves in increasingly dangerous environments and engaging in riskier and riskier drug-taking. Chemsex has seen a surge in popularity in recent years and drugs like GHB – a substance so dangerous that even a drop too much could kill you – is becoming increasingly common on the gay scene, and the death count continues to rise.

I may not have been turning to drugs that night to fill some hole in my life or compensate for past trauma, but that doesn't mean my recreational drug use couldn't turn to addiction, or that I wouldn't one day start using illegal highs to cope with depression or some other underlying mental health issue. Like every single LGBT+ person around the world, I've experienced forms of discrimination throughout my life, and although in many ways I have been so incredibly fortunate, others are not so lucky.

Prejudice follows all of us, and it would be naïve to think that any of us are immune to the consequences of that. Falling victim to substance abuse doesn't make you weak, nor does it make you a failure or a criminal – it makes you a victim of a society that has chewed you up and spat you out, and it could honestly happen to any of us.

Fortunately, Alfie survived that night – but it could've been so much worse. I would see Alfie around a few times over the years that followed, and although I'd like to think that he eventually made a better life for himself, the fact is that he was never truly given the chance that he deserved. He had to struggle for everything that he had, and all of that stemmed from his parents' decision to one day abandon him just because he was gay.

Chapter Twenty-Five

A winter chill cut through the November air as the funeral procession began making its way through the streets. People wore black out of respect and bowed their heads as the pall-bearers struggled under the weight of the coffin. Varsity dutifully stood beside me, her make-up subtle, her glitter and sequins now vanished to give way to a simple and understated black dress. She placed one of her hands on my shoulder as the coffin passed by, and I clutched it as we read the flower arrangement that spelled out the name of the recently deceased: '*Here lies Madame JoJo's, gone but never forgotten.*'

JoJo's had been the latest victim in a long string of closures that saw many of London's most iconic LGBT+ spaces gone for good, and the community had banded together to protest the loss of one of its most beloved bars. Madame JoJo's was more than just a bar; it had been a home to so many – to queer people, to drag queens, to cabaret and burlesque lovers alike. It had been a much-needed community hub, and so it was no surprise that so many piled into the streets to show their support.

Everyone was dressed in sombre clothing and carried signs emblazoned with 'Save Our Soho' as the mock funeral procession marched through the heart of the gay village. A group of mourners wailed with over-the-top theatrics as people stood up one by one to speak passionately about why JoJo's had meant so much to them.

Varsity placed her arm around me and, as I let my community surround me, it reminded me of that night all that time ago in Frankfurt. I'd been at the beginning of my journey, and the Christopher Street Day celebrations had been everything that I needed. I was just a stranger from out of town then, but now I was surrounded by my friends and chosen family.

It was my first protest, but it would be the first of many more to come. That day we protested our bars being closed; tomorrow we'd be demanding access to PrEP, and the next day we'd be campaigning against the atrocities committed by foreign governments. I felt and would feel most at home with my own community, and although our words would often fall on deaf ears, doing something was far better than doing nothing at all.

It was inspiring to see so many people fighting so loudly for something that they believed in, but sadly it wasn't enough. The fight was lost and JoJo's would be closed and demolished, its resident drag queens scattered to new homes across London. It was something that would happen more and more frequently: spaces and venues that meant so much to so many would be closed down at an increasingly alarming rate, from the Black Cap in Camden Town to the Joiners Arms in Hackney. After just a few years, so many of the places I'd grown to love would be closed before my very eyes.

* * *

'So now what?' I said to Varsity as we stood outside Madame JoJo's, its sign finally removed and the building marked for demolition.

'We drink.' She smiled. 'We shan't let it dampen our spirits.' She linked her arm with mine and walked me back down Old Compton Street. 'Do you know what that flag means?' she asked, pointing to the huge flag flying proudly outside the Admiral Duncan.

'It's the rainbow flag?'

'Don't be so dense,' she replied. 'That flag is a mark of defiance. If you walked down here before the turn of the millennium you wouldn't have seen it flying there. You wouldn't have seen any of this.'

'So what changed?' I asked, looking around at the rainbows that surrounded us.

'Three people were killed,' she said. 'Andrea Dykes, Nick Moore and John Light. In that bar right there.' She nodded once more to the Admiral Duncan. 'It was a targeted attack against our community. A nail bomb in 1999. Seventy injured. Three dead.'

'That's awful,' I replied. I was nine at the time, so it would've been well within my living memory, and yet this was the first time I was hearing about it.

'They hung the flag as a message to the world that our community could never be broken, but the council later said that it wasn't allowed, and told them to take it down.'

'And so what happened?'

'They told them to piss off. And then everyone else started hanging up flags as well,' she said, gesturing to the rainbow flags that hung from every window. 'You can't tell queer people what they can and can't do – we're just too stubborn. Tell us we can't do something, and we'll do it just to spite you.'

'And JoJo's?' I asked.

'They can shut down our bars, dear, but they can't shut down our spirits.'

She led me into the Admiral Duncan then, where Ebony and Cindy were performing on the stage inside. They gave a little toast to Madame JoJo's as we entered.

'To JoJo's!' the room cheered in unison.

They were putting on a fundraiser for the Albert Kennedy Trust – a charity that supported homeless LGBT+ youths – and Varsity had offered to come and lend her support.

'Do you want a drink, dear?' she said.

'I'd love one.' I nodded.

'Great, well get me one while you're up there as well, would you?' She winked, pushing me towards the bar before going to join the others up on stage. The three of them took it in turns to entertain the crowd, while the other two held out buckets and encouraged people to dig deep for contributions.

'Apparently it's illegal to shake the bucket,' Varsity said, hopping down off the stage. She walked back towards the bar to join me, shaking the bucket noisily as she did. 'It disturbs the peace or something. I guess they'll just have to arrest me.' She shook the bucket even louder now, and then dangled it in front of a couple, who immediately took out their wallets. 'Thank you, dears, come visit me in prison, won't you?'

'I wish I could do stuff like this,' I said as Varsity finished hounding every person in the room for donations.

'Is there something stopping you, dear?'

'Well no, I guess not, but—'

'It's all very well and good saying you care about this community, but what are you actually going to do about it?' Those words sounded all too familiar; Kuba Chang, Lawaan, even my parents – they'd all said the same thing. Up until then I'd used the excuse that I needed to find my own feet first, but I couldn't use that excuse any more. I'd found my home, the place where I belonged – it was time to give something back.

'You're right,' I said. 'It's just hard to know where to start.'

'Well, what do you think makes us a community?' she asked.

'We all face the same struggles, I guess.'

'Do we, though? Do you really think you share the same struggles as every person in this room?' She gestured around at the diverse patrons who surrounded us.

Gay men, bisexuals, lesbians and trans people. Gender-nonconforming and non-binary people. People of all ages, people of colour and people of faith. People with disabilities and people living with HIV. Drag queens, parents, sex workers and teachers.

People who'd lost their homes.

People who'd lost a friend.

'It's our differences that bring us together, not our similarities,' she said. 'There's no one single way to help or solve the plight of the entire community. If you really want to help, you have to do it one person at a time.'

I thought on that for a moment and thought about all the people who had helped me when I'd needed them. No matter where I was in the world, I never felt alone, and that was thanks to my community. To Matteo, Jack, Carmen, Vibhor, Lawaan, Ying, Freddie and Varsity. They were just a few of the people who had reached out a hand of support – I'd been a stranger to all of them, and yet they'd each welcomed me into their unique little worlds without a second thought.

I realised then that being LGBT+ is the single greatest gift that's ever been given to me – because no matter what, I knew I would never be on my own. I'd spent so long looking for a place to call home, but that home had been in front of me all along. Home for me was right here with my community, and it didn't matter where I was in the world, because they'd always be right there beside me. I made a promise to myself then that I would find a way to give back, not by expecting to solve all the world's problems with some big sweeping gesture, but rather with the day-to-day kindnesses that our community is built upon.

We spent the rest of the evening popping in and out of Soho's various gay bars. We said a cheers to Madame JoJo's in every bar we went in, our toasts becoming more and more slurred as the night went on – a final hoorah for the bar where we'd first met.

It must've been 4 a.m. by the time we finally stumbled out onto the streets, in search of something to eat. Varsity caught me as I fell out of a doorway on Old Compton Street, the gentle pitter-patter of rain starting to fall all around us.

We were entirely alone, save for a young gay couple just turning the corner up ahead of us, hoods pulled tightly over their heads to shield them from the rain as they huddled together and clung to one another for warmth.

'Adorable, isn't it?' Varsity said, leaning her head into mine as we watched the two boys disappear down the side street.

'Yeah.' I smiled. 'It's beautiful.'

'Breakfast?' she said, gesturing to our favourite 24-hour restaurant as we took one final walk down the Soho Catwalk, the 4 a.m. streetlights reflecting in the wet pavement as the rainbows billowed on either side of us.

'Breakfast.' I nodded, and quietly followed her inside.

Epilogue

'Some people are trans, get over it!' one of the placards read as I joined the sea of people gathering beneath the giant rainbow of acceptance, diversity and inclusion.

It was the summer of 2015, and over a million people flocked to the streets to celebrate Pride in London. I watched on as old friends gleefully jumped into each other's arms, young couples walked proudly hand in hand and families gathered to show support for the people they loved. It was the largest Pride I'd ever attended – the largest the UK had ever seen – and it was a special day for me personally, because it was the first time I had the privilege of walking in the parade.

'Pride is a protest!' I chorused with the procession as we marched through the streets and confetti rained all around us. For just one day, the city was united in its acceptance of love and freedom of expression, and it's a moment that I know will stay with me for ever. I was there to represent Stonewall – they were one of the many incredible LGBT+ organisations I had the pleasure of working with – and in doing so I had found that fulfilment that I'd been in search of for so long. By finally using my voice and speaking out about more of the issues that mattered to me, I discovered the thing that surprised me more than anything – that people were actually willing to listen.

I'd come such a tremendously long way from the beginnings of my journey, but I couldn't help but think back to the first Pride I ever attended. It had been eight years since Shaun Dykes had tragically lost his life, and I only wished that he could have been there to see how drastically our world had changed. In those eight short years, we'd seen enormous LGBT+ advancements that spanned right across the globe.

It's important to take these moments to remind ourselves how far we've come, but we also owe it to people like Shaun to remember that, until the day we achieve true global equality, our fight is not yet won. Things are indeed improving and yet there still isn't a single country in the world where LGBT+ people are treated as equals in every aspect of life – whether that's same-sex couples being unable to adopt in Italy; gay marriage being prohibited in India; or trans people still being denied the right to legally change their gender in Thailand.

Even here in the UK there are still many inequalities that affect us – from the inequality of the rights of gay and bisexual men when it comes to donating blood, to non-binary people being unable to obtain legal documentation to reflect their gender identity, or trans people still being unable to access the healthcare they need.

I believe we are at a sensitive turning point in history – LGBT+ rights have come along further in the past few decades than they have in the centuries that preceded them, but our basic human rights seem to still be considered as up for discussion, and our freedoms appear to be decided upon in the court of public opinion. Debate still rages on over whether LGBT+ inclusive education should be taught in our schools; trans people are at the centre of an unprecedented media onslaught; and the number of hate crimes committed against LGBT+ people continues to rise.

But in spite of these alarming facts, there *is* still hope. In the time it's taken me to write this book, the number of countries where it's illegal to be gay has dropped from seventy-eight to seventy-three, and with LGBT+ activists and organisations working tirelessly around the globe, by the time you're actually reading this that number could have dropped even further still.

I have every hope that this progress will continue, and seeing the embodiment of that hope every year at Pride is what truly keeps me believing in this wonderful community. There is nothing more inspiring than seeing people half my age proudly thrusting their rainbow flags high into the air to stand up for what they believe in.

Gilbert Baker designed that flag in hope of a brighter tomorrow, and it's a flag that still brings together our community and unifies us under the colours of the rainbow. To some, it may just be a few colours twisting in the wind, but to me it's a reminder of the millions of incredible people that our community is made up of.

It's long drives with Freddie along the seafront, sharing a bottle of Thums Up with Vibhor, playing capture-the-flag with Giovanni and Matteo, or slipping backstage at Varsity's drag show. It's the comfort of Lawaan's guesthouse, the warmth of Ying's kind smile, the hand of friendship from Carmen, or a kiss goodbye from Jack.

I remember a time, before I met these people, when I felt like I didn't belong – and I know there are so many people out there who still feel that way today. It's for that reason that I wanted to share these stories – I've kept them to myself for many years, sharing them only with the people closest to me, but I'm hoping, in telling them now, that they can serve as a reminder that none of us can ever really be alone, because the world is full of LGBT+ people just like us.

If there's one thing I've learned from writing this book, it's that it's through being inspired by others – as I was – that we're able to keep progressing forwards. So live boldly and bravely, and never apologise for being yourself.

There's power in the love and kindness that we share with each other, and it's in those moments that our community truly thrives.

Resources

This book brushes up against some incredibly complex issues that I know many people will be affected by. If you are one of them or know someone who is, or you aren't but would like to learn more, I've included a short list of some of the LGBT+ organisations and helplines that are working towards providing information, advice and support to people who need them. These are just a few of the many incredible LGBT+ organisations out there, and while it's not a complete or exhaustive list, groups like Stonewall will be able to point you towards resources for further support.

Organisations & charities

Stonewall

Named after the Stonewall Riots that took place in New York City in 1969, Stonewall is an organisation that works tirelessly towards making the world a better place for LGBT+ people everywhere. It is the largest LGBT+ rights organisation in Europe, and a great starting point for anyone looking to learn more about the issues that affect our community.

Website: www.stonewall.org.uk

Terrence Higgins Trust
As the UK's leading HIV and sexual health charity, Terrence Higgins Trust works towards supporting people living with HIV, eradicating stigma and discrimination, and ending new transmissions. I had the enormous pleasure of working at Terrence Higgins Trust between 2014 and 2018, and can't advocate any more highly for the incredible work they do.
Website: www.tht.org.uk

Albert Kennedy Trust
Working towards supporting LGBT+ young people, the Albert Kennedy Trust offer help and support to those aged 16–25 who are experiencing homelessness or living in a hostile environment. LGBT+ young people are far more likely to find themselves homeless, making up to 24% of the youth homeless population, and so the charity's work is absolutely vital.
Website: www.akt.org.uk
Phone: 020 7831 6562

Friday/Monday
Produced by Terrence Higgins Trust, this resource provides information about sex and drugs for gay and bisexual men, from detailed information on the different types of drugs and their effects, to advice on getting help and support on various issues, such as chemsex.
Website: www.fridaymonday.org.uk

Galop
As the UK's main specialist LGBT+ anti-violence charity, Galop provide advice, support and advocacy to people who have experienced hate crimes, domestic abuse and sexual violence. With a commitment to always making their support services both free and confidential, their mission is to make life just, fair and safe

for LGBT+ people across the country.
Website: www.galop.org.uk

Mermaids UK

Mermaids UK is one of the UK's leading LGBT+ charities, and they work towards supporting and empowering trans and gender-diverse children and their families. They believe that transgender children deserve the freedom and confidence to explore their gender identity wherever their journey takes them, free from fear, isolation, and discrimination.
Website: mermaidsuk.org.uk

Helplines

Switchboard

(Mon to Sun: 10am–10pm)
Providing calm words when they're needed most, Switchboard is a confidential LGBT+ helpline that provides information and support to anyone who needs it.
Website: switchboard.lgbt
Phone: 0300 330 0630

Mermaids Helpline

(Mon to Fri: 9am–9pm)
Mermaids' helpline is confidential and available for transgender youth up to the age of 19, as well as their families and any professionals working with them.
Website: mermaidsuk.org.uk/contact-us
Phone: 0808 801 0400

Terrence Higgins Trust Direct Helpline

(Mon to Fri: 10am–8pm)
A confidential support service for issues related to HIV or sexual health. They're available to offer advice and information and

can help you to find and access sexual health services.
Phone: 0808 802 1221

National LGBT+ Domestic Abuse Helpline
(Mon to Fri: 10am–5pm; Wed to Thu: 10am–8pm)
Providing support for LGBT+ people experiencing domestic abuse. Abuse isn't always physical, it can be psychological, emotional, financial and sexual too. Don't suffer in silence.
Phone: 0800 999 5428

London LGBT+ Advice Line
(Mon to Fri: 10am–12.30pm, 1.30pm–4pm)
For any issues relating to LGBT+ violence, this advice and support line is available specifically for LGBT+ people living in London.
Phone: 020 7704 2040

Acknowledgements

First and foremost, I'd like to thank all the incredible people whom this book is based upon. Thank you for your friendship and for giving me the opportunity to tell these stories – all of the wonderful LGBT+ people mentioned in this book have changed my life for the better, and I'm eternally grateful for every single moment I got to spend with them.

Thank you to Ella Kahn, my wonderful literary agent, for believing in this book before I'd even put pen to paper; to the team at Hodder & Stoughton for taking a chance on this story; and to Ian Wong, my editor, for providing such thoughtful edits and suggestions – it has truly meant the world to have another LGBT+ person working on this book with me, and your knowledge and insight have proved instrumental to making this book a far better one than what I could have achieved without you.

Thank you to my parents and my late grandmother for always believing in me, for providing a safe and loving environment in which to thrive, and for encouraging my dreams of being a published author since I was small; to Laura Jane Williams for offering to lend me a pen when I first sat next to you in our first writing class, and for the twelve years of friendship that followed;

and to Melanie Murphy, Doug Armstrong, Roly West, and Olly Pike for being incredibly patient and supportive throughout the writing process. Whenever I wanted to throw my laptop out of the window with frustration, you were the ones to constantly remind me that I *could* do this and wouldn't let me give up.

Thank you to Matthew Todd for first taking me on as an intern at *Attitude* magazine in 2010 and encouraging me to find my feet as a writer. You have been both a friend and a mentor to me over the years, and I only aspire to one day be able to write LGBT+ stories as well as you do.

Thank you to Kush Khanna and Andrea Di Giovanni for providing such needed insight into some of the cultural issues explored in these pages (and for correcting my terrible Italian!) and to Asifa Lahore and Ferhan Khan for the conversations that helped me to see things from a new perspective.

Thank you to Elizabeth Gilbert for writing *Eat, Pray, Love* — reading those words as a teenager inspired my love of people and travel, and without them I'm not sure I'd have ever found the confidence to start the journey that I did. It only seems fitting that your work would now also inspire the title for my first book.

Thank you also to all of the amazing LGBT+ activists and organisations who are working tirelessly around the globe to win our freedoms – without you, I wouldn't be in the position to be able to write a book like this one.

And finally, and arguably most importantly, to all of my incredible supporters who have followed me for the past ten years. Since *Eat, Gay, Love* first came into the world as a written blog in 2010 and later a video blog in 2013, you have been with me throughout this entire journey and supported me every single step of the way. You made all of this possible and I truly can't wait to share more stories with you.

Thank you. x